RIDE FROM WITHIN

RIDE FROM WITHIN

Use Tai Chi Principles to Awaken Your Natural Balance and Rhythm

James Shaw

with **Christopher Bray**
and **Charlene Strickland**

TRAFALGAR SQUARE PUBLISHING
NORTH POMFRET, VT

First published in 2005 by

Trafalgar Square Publishing
North Pomfret, Vermont 05053

Printed in China

Library of Congress Cataloging-in-Publication Data

Shaw, James, 1961-
  Ride from within : use tai chi principles to awaken your natural balance and rhythm / James Shaw.
     p. cm.
  Includes index.
  ISBN-13: 978-1-57076-318-2 (pbk.)
  ISBN-10: 1-57076-318-6 (pbk.)
  1. Horsemanship—Psychological aspects. 2. Tai chi. I. Title.

  SF309.S535 2005
  798.2—dc22

                                        2005005827

Illustration Credits:
Photos: Dean Goodwin (page 6); Kristi Smythe (pages 26, 55, 57–60, 105, 110, 134–5, 161 *top and bottom right*); James Shaw (28,181); Joe Torrino (pages 38–9, 45, 47, 52–3, 62, 70–1, 91–2 *right*, 103, 107–8, 122–3, 125, 127–8, 130, 133, 139, 141, 143, 147, 151–2, 155, 159–160, 161 *bottom left,* 193); Merrily Veatch (pages 40, 92 *left,* 93); Mandy Lorraine, courtesy of Betsy Steiner (page 176); phelpsphotos.com, courtesy of Betsy Steiner (pages 186, 192, 203, 210)
Line Art: James Shaw (page 3); Brenda Gountis (pages 19, 21, 25–6, 84, 86–8, 101, 112, 119, 144, 148, 177, 180, 188, 194, 199, 211); Heather Mansfield (pages 246–250)

Book design by Carrie Fradkin
Cover design by Heather Mansfield
Typeface: Rotis Sans, Rotis Serif, Modern No. 20, and Syntax

10 9 8 7 6 5 4 3 2 1

To my son Liam

Born one month after the agreement was made to write this book and inspiring me to take the first step of the journey into the life of my wildest dreams. The love I feel for you fills me in a way that I never dreamed possible. It is that abundance of love that moves me through the fears and doubts that come with living wild dreams. I hope, in turn, I inspire you to live your dreams.

And to my parents Edward & Alice Shaw

My mom, who gave me my first and greatest gift: life. You have been a shining example of how to live and embrace the adventure of Life. We've come a long way from the miracle of tenth-grade English class.

My dad: We had far too short a time together in this life. I feel your presence near me often and I hope I've made you proud.

"A good traveler has no fixed plans
and is not intent on arriving."

—Lao Tzu, *Tao Te Ching*

Table of Contents

Preface

True wisdom endures and remains timelessly relevant. You are about to begin a profound journey of learning and discovery in which you will encounter a 4,000-year-old art that is still wise, still relevant, and entirely vital.

In centuries past, horse ownership and training, as well as instruction in riding, were often limited to society's elite. Today these pursuits have become accessible to people from all walks of life, and an ever-growing number of riders now have the opportunity to experience the unparalleled sensations of flow, strength, and connection that one can feel upon the back of a horse—an astoundingly beautiful and powerful animal.

In ancient China, Tai Chi was only available to the elite. Today, Tai Chi has become widely accessible and millions of people now practice this art. Tai Chi unifies the body, mind, and spirit in a series of flowing movements that align the posture, breath, and the inner and outermost being. This ancient art offers a path to becoming more completely alive and more fully conscious.

Bringing together horsemanship and Tai Chi makes great sense and provides riders with a wonderful opportunity. Tai Chi can open the doors to deep experiences for horsemen, both on and off the horse. Learning to ride well requires us to be conscious equestrians, but this means that we must first be *self*-conscious. *To become one with your horse you must first become one with yourself*—this is the journey of this book.

On this voyage, your mind and breath will take you deep into your body's center, to discover the origins of connection as well as those of disconnection—the imbalances and tensions that separate you from your inner self and from your horse. You will also find the roots of power, which you will learn to apply to your riding. You will become more centered in your body and calm in your mind. Most importantly, you will gain control over your breathing, so that you stay connected in mind and body.

As you gain Tai Chi skills and experiences and apply them to your riding, you will find your horsemanship becoming not just more skilled, but more deeply satisfying on a level that transcends language and even time. You and your horse will simply be.

Note to the Reader

Why and How to Use This Book

To guide you along the path of mind, breath, and body, I introduce the fundamentals of Tai Chi in the early chapters and then include a variety of exercises in chapters 3 through 6. These chapters form a program, with exercises building upon the teachings and personal experiences you have just learned. In chapter 6, you'll apply the skills and awareness you've gained from the exercises to your riding.

Using step-by-step instruction and pictures, I coach you through the essentials of Tai Chi for the equestrian. The exercises generally include both unmounted and mounted versions. The unmounted exercises are based on Tai Chi forms, specifically adapted to prepare you for in-the-saddle exercises. On pages 240–243 in the *Appendix* you can see a detailed summary of all the exercises, which outlines their purpose, the routine to be followed, and when to move on.

The exercises are presented as follows:

Riding Goals list the goals of each exercise and the benefits that will carry over to your riding.

Function previews how the exercise will change your mind, breath, and body.

Intent suggests ways to use your mind to help you focus on the exercise.

Step-by-Step gives you a breakdown of the movements.

You'll find instructions for both unmounted and mounted phases. Some exercises are only on the ground, although you'll carry over these new abilities into the saddle.

Ah-Ha! shares insights about what you'll experience when you practice correctly. These feelings let you know you're succeeding.

Ability Transition includes tips to keep you advancing. Practicing an exercise helps you make progress.

Reminders present cautions to help you avoid the pitfalls that I most commonly see when people are learning a new movement.

James On Your Shoulder provides you, on occasion, with supplementary ideas to help improve your practice and enrich your understanding of it. Think of me as standing right behind you, or sitting behind you as you ride, offering suggestions and inspiration.

Benefits You'll Experience through the Exercise Program

Benefit	*What You'll Experience*
• Improved mind–body connection	All your actions will be directed by your mind. You will begin to sense what your horse is going to do before it happens.
• Enhanced mobility in all your joints	The movement in your body will become smoother, more sensitive, and better controlled, and your range of motion will increase.
• Heightened sensitivity	You will feel more of your horse's movements in your seat and hands and be able to adjust to those changes without over compensating.
• Relaxed, consistent breathing	You will always know where your breath is and that you are not holding it.
• Expanded awareness	You will hear, feel, and see more when you're riding, leading to a deeper connection with your horse.
• Improved balance	You will discover and change imbalances in you and your horse before they adversely affect your connection.
• Improved health	With regular practice, you will feel stronger in your body and calmer in your mind. You will experience improved energy and endurance.

Tai Chi and Horsemanship

1

I N THIS FIRST CHAPTER, I LAY THE GROUNDWORK for the rest of this book. You learn about what Tai Chi—both as a philosophy and a martial art—offers you as a rider, and you are introduced to the systems of thinking underlying Tai Chi, including Yin and Yang, Tao, and Tai Chi's connection with horsemanship. In addition, you learn what enrichments you can expect from making Tai Chi part of your riding practice.

Tai Chi: Riding with Life's Energy, Connecting with Your Horse

Through Tai Chi you will achieve a true connection by learning to *join centers* with your horse. When joined, you match the rhythm of your center to that of your horse. You actively control the movements of your entire body, not just your arms and legs. You develop your balance independent of your horse. If you rely on your horse for balance, your horse is in control of your center; if your horse relies on you for his balance, then you are in control of your horse's center.

Tai Chi teaches you to stay centered by controlling your position and motion. Control grows from a strengthened mind-body foundation, in which you develop a perfect state of awareness. This awareness allows you to detect instantly any change of balance, either in yourself or your horse, and compensate for it without ever losing your rhythm. Your mind directs your body, and your body follows. You soon discover that your mind directs not only your body, but also your horse.

Tai Chi as a *philosophy* or *spiritual practice* abounds with unseen forces and energies that are often difficult to comprehend or explain. Tai Chi as a *martial art*, in contrast, is bound by well-known and well-understood laws of physics. I assume that the natural laws of physics apply to riding, and that is the perspective from which I have written this book. I have, however, seen things happen while working with a horse and rider that are difficult to explain in exclusively scientific terms.

Chi means "energy" or "life force," and in Tai Chi, you direct the flow of your chi with your mind. Because some practitioners of Tai Chi believe that there are no limits to the mind's capabilities, they also believe that this art can extend beyond what we can explain through our usual understanding of our everyday world. While this book will limit its approach and instructions to the world of natural law, I can confidently tell you that you are very likely to find your practice of Tai Chi occasionally going beyond ordinary experience. Rather than label these experiences or debate their nature, I suggest we simply enjoy them as part of the daily miracle that we call life. We will discuss chi in much greater depth in the next chapter.

The Yin Yang Perspective

From Tai Chi, which means, literally, "great ultimate," arise Yin and Yang, the fundamental, equal and opposite forces that underlie the ever-changing cycles of the universe. Complementary and inseparable, these two powers constantly balance each other. Everything in the universe derives its existence from the balanced interaction of Yin and Yang. You can see this interaction in the apparent opposites in our world—summer and winter, night and day, hot and cold, male and female.

The idea of balancing two natural forces has been a constant throughout Chinese history, whether it refers to the way of the universe, the martial art of Tai Chi, or the balance between horse and rider. The idea of Yin and Yang is also at the foundation of this book and my teaching method. By applying this theory to riding, you can discover a wealth of information and techniques to improve your connection with the horse.

When I look at a horse and rider, I see them as one organic whole—one whole in which two separate entities or forces can join synergistically, and the whole becomes greater than the sum of its parts. If there is an imbalance in either part, the whole is imbalanced. By changing one, we change the other. When the two join in balance, there is a flow and power like that of a great river moving through a mountain gorge.

The Tai Chi symbol is often referred to as the Yin and Yang. The Yin (soft, female, light) and Yang (hard, male, heavy) applies not only to horse and rider but also to the entire human body. Tai Chi Master Chang San-Feng wrote in the *Tai Chi Classics*, "When the entire body is integrated with all parts connected together, it becomes a vast connection of positive and negative energy units. Each positive and negative unit should be connected to every other unit and permitted no interruption among them."

For example, when moving forward, the *front* of your body is considered positive or Yang, and the *back* negative or Yin. Furthermore, if you are pushing your hand forward with the palm out, the palm is considered Yang, and the back of the hand Yin. In relationship to the whole arm, the hand is Yang, and the arm Yin. If the left hand is moving forward (Yang), the right hand is Yin. Neither positive nor negative can act independently; all body parts and all movements are relative.

Yin and Yang: A Horse Story

I was once asked by a friend to come out to her barn and help her horse's movement: his inside hind foot was not tracking up, that is, not stepping forward far enough to fall in the foot print of the inside front.

As I stood in the middle of the arena watching her and a magnificent stallion circle

The Chinese character Chi, meaning breath energy, life force, and air.

The Tai Chi symbol, more commonly known as the Yin and Yang symbol, represents the principle of balance in the universe.

around me, my first thought was, "How incredibly connected they both are." My second thought was, "How can I help improve the trot of a world-class rider and equally talented horse?" The answer was to see them as Yin and Yang on a small scale and know that they were bound by the same natural laws.

My next thought was that if there were more weight to the inside of the circle, it could cause the horse to put his hind foot down sooner, not allowing it to travel as far forward. I had to find out whether or not this added weight came from the rider or the horse.

Applying the theory of Yin and Yang, I reasoned that if one side is heavy the other must be light, so I asked my friend to imagine a 5-pound weight in her outside hand as she rode on the circle. Within one revolution, the inside hind foot of her horse moved a full 6 inches forward and was now tracking up beautifully.

The rider's success was directly related to her ability to weight her hand subtly without compromising the fluid motion of the rest of her body. That's not an easy task at the walk, let alone at the trot. The insight that directed us to the root of the problem and the solution was an understanding of Yin and Yang principles.

Tao

If Yin and Yang are the parts, the Tao is the whole. "Tao" means many things to many people, and its meaning goes beyond words. Ancient texts describe the Tao tangentially, developing their definitions through sayings, stories, and allegories. The concept of Tao is difficult to fathom with a Western mind. For me, defining the Tao is like asking someone from the West to describe God definitively. What would she say? "He/She/It is every-where, the beginning and the end, the cause and director of all life"?

The following words describing Tao were inscribed on a Ming rock dated 1556. In trying to grasp the concept of Tao, it may be helpful to replace the word "Tao" with "God." Read it with an open mind and a God of your own understanding.

> Vast indeed is the Ultimate Tao,
> Spontaneously itself, apparently without acting,
> End of all ages and beginning of all ages,
> Existing before Earth and existing before Heaven,
> Silently embracing the whole of time,

Continuing uninterrupted through all eons,

In the east it taught Father Confucius,

In the west it converted the Golden man [the Buddha],

Taken as pattern by a hundred kings,

Transmitted by generations of sages,

It is the ancestor of all doctrines,

The mystery beyond all mysteries.[1]

Lao Tzu, a contemporary of Confucius, was keeper of the imperial archives at Loyang in the province of Honan in the sixth century BC. Acknowledging the profundity of this concept, Lao Tzu said, "The Tao that can be told is not the eternal Tao."

According to ancient legend, as Lao Tzu was riding off into the desert to die, sick at heart at the ways of men, he was persuaded to write down his teachings for posterity. The work he created, the *Tao Te Ching*, captures the essence of Taoism in only five thousand words. For over 2500 years this book has been one of the greatest influences on Chinese thought and culture.

Tai Chi exercise is born of the Yin and Yang, and "The mother of Yin and Yang is Tao." Lao Tzu put it this way in the *Tao Te Ching*:

The Tao that can be told is not the eternal Tao.

The name that can be named is not the eternal name.

The nameless is the beginning of heaven and earth.

The named is the mother of ten thousand things.[2]

I interpret that passage in this way:

The Tao that can be told is not the eternal Tao.

The name that can be named (Tai Chi) is not the eternal name (Tao).

The nameless (Tao) is the beginning of heaven and earth (Yin and Yang).

The named (Tai Chi) is the mother of ten thousand things (Universe).

Lao Tzu continues:

Under heaven and earth all can see beauty as beauty only because there is ugliness.

All can know good as good only because there is evil.

Therefore having and not having arise together.

1 Rawson, Philip and Legeza, Laszlo. *Tao: The Chinese Philosophy of Time and Change.* London: Thames and Hudson, 1973.

2 Feng, Gia-Fu, and English, Jane, trans. *Tao Te Ching.* New York: Random House, 1972.

Difficult and easy complement each other.

Long and short contrast each other.

High and low rest upon each other.

Voice and sound harmonize each other.

Front and back follow one another.

Tai Chi, Horsemanship, and the Laws of Nature

Tai Chi and horsemanship share a long, rich history. Horsemanship dates back approximately 6000 years, and horses played important and revered roles in the feudal society of ancient China. Over thousands of years, the dynasties of the Shang, Chou, Han,

Ming horse

T'ang, Ming, Ch'ing and others created a rich and splendid culture. They all developed the arts and sciences, and they all waged war. Throughout these millennia, horses helped the dynasties thrive, in peace and in war, and stories and images of horses are woven into the fabric of Chinese culture. Their high esteem is reflected in the honor accorded them by their burial in royal tombs dating from the 14th century BC.

Horsemanship, like Tai Chi, embodies centuries of wisdom passed from generation to generation, perpetuated by masters instructing students, the best of whom become the next generation's masters. In this way, the tenets of horsemanship have survived, inculcated through direct instruction and codified in classic manuals such as Xenophon's *The Art of Horsemanship*, written over 2000 years ago, or Pluvinel's *Le Maneige Royal*, written almost 400 years ago. In this way, knowledge of the art, as well as its humanity, has survived across time.

The forms of Tai Chi relate closely to the practice of horsemanship. A skilled rider communicates thoughts that become the actions of the horse. Horsemanship and Tai Chi also share concepts of mind and body control. Through the practice of Tai Chi, you learn to take advantage of, and stay in harmony with, the laws of nature. The influence of these forces on you and your horse should not be underestimated. Whether you recognize them or not, these forces and your response to them determine whether or not you are in or out of rhythm with your horse. Because you can't escape these laws of physics, you need to learn how to use them to enhance your riding—and that is what we will do in chapter 2. But first, I want to introduce the four principal forces affecting you as a rider: they are *gravity*, *momentum*, *tension*, and *centripetal force*.

Gravity

When talking about natural laws, gravity is the king. Ever-present and unyielding, gravity can be either your tiring nemesis or your tireless friend. Understanding gravity is the first step to making it your friend.

Most people have spent their entire lives moving within this constant force without ever fully understanding its effects on human movement and health. Space travel, for example, has proven that gravity has a positive effect on our bones. During periods of extended weightlessness, when skeletons no longer have to resist gravity, an astronaut's bones lose density and strength. Gravity provides us with continual, necessary exercise.

Life on earth requires us to "stand up to" the constant force of gravity, and we use our bones and muscles to accomplish this. If we align our skeletons with the force of gravity, then our bones can passively support much of our weight and our muscles have an easier job, as they only have to work to maintain the alignment of our skeleton. If we lose that alignment, then our muscles have to work harder to support us because they are forced to actively carry some of the load that our bones can carry passively.

You already know this intuitively: if you have to pick up something heavy, you pick it up closer to your body (in alignment with your spine, thereby maximizing the load on your bones), not out at arm's length, where the effort becomes almost entirely muscular.

In the same way, riding starts with your foundation, with "picking up," supporting, and balancing your body. To achieve this balance in the saddle, you employ your muscles and skeleton. The more you maintain the alignment of your skeleton, the less muscular effort you must use for balance, which translates into less tension and fatigue and more relaxation and better connection with your horse. You can then take advantage of the tremendous power of *momentum*.

Momentum

Using momentum is the key to being able to direct your horse's force, which is far greater than your own, with minimal effort. The relationship between you and momen-

Tai Chi's Origins

Tai Chi means "the great ultimate." It is both a Chinese martial art and a way of life. Among the ancient Chinese arts, Tai Chi was an internal art, a metaphysical concept. Master Chang San-Feng wrote in the *Tai Chi Classics*, "Tai Chi became the invisible power that guided the movements of Chinese history for thousands of years. It gave tremendous impetus to that fabulous culture, showing its influence in areas ranging from medicine to diet, from art to economics." Tai Chi is a discipline inspired by the Taoist philosophy. As philosophies of idealism, both Tai Chi and Taoism unite the body with the mind, so the individual lives in harmony with nature.

The author practicing Tai Chi

While no one knows exactly when Tai Chi coalesced into a formal system, most historians date its founding to approximately 2000 BC. The art has grown and evolved in different ways, shaped by its practitioners. Tai Chi has often been affected by political systems, such as when authoritarian regimes saw Tai Chi as a weapon and developed it as a fighting art for nobles and warriors. Taoists and other intellectuals, however, remaining independent of the political structures of the dynasties, emphasized Tai Chi's more metaphysical aspects. The Taoist monk Chang San-Feng, for example, established in AD 1200 an internal system of pure art, in contrast to the external, martial art practiced by the ruling class. Regardless of each practice's emphasis or origins, the pedagogy was similar: masters tutored students who became disciples of the art, and some of these students went on to become masters themselves.

Under the Ch'ing (Manchu) dynasty (AD 1644–1912), Tai Chi was a sophisticated and highly developed art that continued to evolve both as a martial art and as an intellectual discipline that included the philosophy of natural harmony. During this period, three principal styles of Tai Chi emerged: the original Chen style and two offshoots, the Yang and Wu. The Yang style was founded by Yang Lu-Chang, a famous martial arts master. Yang instructed Chuan You, whose son, Master Wu Chian-chuan (1870–1940) went on to found the Wu style.

The Wu style focuses on smooth, even, continuous motions, and it is the inspiration for Tai Chi for the equestrian. Master Wu himself established the connection between Tai Chi and riding: "[Wu] was also good at horse-riding and shooting and could hide himself under the saddle of a horse or stand on his head on the back of a horse when it was running fast."[3]

When the nearly 300-year-old Ch'ing dynasty ended in 1912 with the founding of the Republic of China, Tai Chi evolved once again. The Yang and Wu styles became available to the public through the Athletic Research Institute in Peking, where Master Wu became one of the teachers. In 1928, Master Wu moved to Shanghai to continue his teachings, and in 1935 he founded the Chian-chuan Taichichuan Association. The Association has helped to spread the Wu style throughout China and around the world.

Common to all these styles are the *forms*, a sequence of slow movements that incorporate aspects of the martial arts, body soundness, and meditation. In a form, the student joins deliberate movements with a tranquility of mind, and action follows thought.

3 Ma Yueh-liang, et al. *Wu Style Tai Chi Chuan*, Berkeley: North Atlantic Books, 2002.

tum is like that between waves and the ocean. The energy (momentum) of a wave created by a hurricane can travel thousands of miles before it crashes into the shoreline. The energy does not move or transport the water itself these thousands of miles; the energy moves *through* the water. Waves of momentum created by the horse move through your body. When you relax, becoming "fluid" (like water!), you allow the wave of horse-generated energy to move through you, unrestricted by tension, and your body remains quiet and still.

As a rider, you can harness the power of momentum. You give your most effective aids when you take advantage of your own momentum. Think about giving an aid with your seat while trotting. The most advantageous time to apply the aid is when the momentum of your body, dropping with the saddle (the horse's center), reaches the lowest point in the fall of your "joined centers." If you give the aid too early, you cut its effectiveness dramatically. Without momentum on your side, you must use your leg to drive the horse on; what should have been the joined forward flow of energy now becomes, instead, the disjointed movements of a horse and rider pair that are no longer in full harmony.

To tap into the power of your momentum you must first match the rhythm of your body to that of your horse. Without this harmony of motion, you will lack the timing necessary to take advantage of the innate power of your momentum.

Just as a lack of timing works against the effortless application of momentum in your riding, unnecessary *tension* in your body works to keep you separated from the power of your horse. This is one of those cases of "If it (the horse's power) is not working for you, it's working against you."

Tension

Tension is the condition of exerting force against one's self, pitting one muscle against another. Tension is apparent when you are "holding" yourself in balance, or when you brace any part of your body prior to giving an aid.

Tension disrupts and disconnects the body from the natural power of momentum. Momentum cannot flow through tense muscles, though it will move *past* tense muscles regardless. Again think of a wave moving through the ocean. When the wave encounters an iceberg (tension), the wave does not flow through it. Instead the wave lifts, tilts, and jostles the berg as it moves past.

Waves of momentum moving through a tense body upset its balance in the same way. The unbalanced body then becomes even tenser, including the seat, thereby reducing the rider's effectiveness, and leaving the rider even more vulnerable to further unbalancing by the next wave of energy from the horse. The solution to this deteriorating situation is first to align your bones. This will reduce the tension in your body and relax your mind. As a result, you will recover your natural balance and ride in relaxation—both mentally and physically. A relaxed mind creates a state of calmness in which your mind is acutely aware of your body. And, a relaxed body has muscles that are free of any unnecessary tension.

Thus far we have looked at the role of gravity that pulls on us constantly, momentum that generates power we can harness, tension that can interfere with our connection with the horse, and now we'll look at the last major force that influences our riding: *centripetal force.*

Centripetal Force

A fundamental law of physics observes that objects travel forward in a straight line at constant speed unless acted on by another force. When centripetal (center-seeking) force is applied to an object traveling in a straight line, the object begins to move on a circle rather than straight ahead. For example, when a parent holds a child's hands and spins the child in a circle, the parent not only moves the child forward, but also pulls the child in. This "pulling in" is centripetal force. Its complement is centrifugal (center-fleeing) force—the "pulling out" force exerted on the parent by the child.

When you and your horse ride a circle, your horse plays the role of the parent, and you the child. On a left lead, for instance, with every stride, your horse not only carries you forward, but also pulls you a little to the left and inside. When he does this over and over again, you complete a circle.

As a rider, however, you may feel more that you are "falling to the outside" than being "pulled to the inside." Because your body's constant tendency is to move straight ahead, while your horse is moving ahead and to the inside, you are, relative to your horse, "falling to the outside."

Regardless of whether we focus on the physics or your perceptions, centripetal force is always at work when you and your horse turn—and it may unbalance you. Using Tai

Chi, you do not need to fight centripetal force; you learn to compensate for it and maintain your soft, balanced seat—your foundation. (For a more in-depth look at centripetal force, see page 213.)

Tai Chi, You, and Your Horse

As you have already begun to learn, Tai Chi is about developing your self and then using that more developed self to enhance your riding. Your improvement as a rider will affect your horse's performance. You won't try to change your horse *directly*, but rather *indirectly* by changing your balance. In my experience, the horse changes dramatically when the rider's balance improves.

Before we go on, let's consider your current situation. While there are many levels at which you and I may communicate with horses—mentally, physically, and spiritually— the moment that you climb on your horse's back, none of those forms of communication speaks louder than the physical. Do you move in harmony and rhythm with your horse? Or, do you sense that through imbalance and tension you get in the way of his natural balance and flow? Are you asking your horse for one thing with your mind and spirit, but telling him something else with your body?

When you ride, you may confront challenges that feel like problems. Can you identify with any of these?

- A lack of harmony or feeling out of rhythm with your horse.
- Conflicts that feel like a tug-o-war, either physical or mental.
- Flashes of connecting with your horse that seem to vanish as soon as you realize they've occurred.
- Fear that your horse may misbehave.
- Fear that you may fall and possibly be injured.
- Frustration because your horse is not listening to you.

In the chapters that follow, I'll investigate ways to diffuse these issues. Tai Chi will help you solve your problems, improve your riding, and develop a more intimate relationship with your horse.

Instructions and Rider Insights

Each chapter of this book contains a series of comfortable, straightforward steps in which you will learn Tai Chi techniques that enable you, regardless of your current riding level or discipline, to advance. At first these exercises may seem a bit daunting, yet as I guide you through the simple, step-by-step instructions, I can assure you that you *will learn*—at the levels of mind, body, and spirit.

In addition to me as your guide, in *Rider Insights* you will hear the helpful stories of many other riders with whom I've worked. These riders faced the same issues you face, and they'll share their experiences with you.

Before we begin, listen to several other riders who have also started down this same path.

Rider Insight, Laura: "I can't tell you how cool it was! I had an epiphany. My body fell into place just as James said it would, and I was riding an awesome canter half-pass. Even better, as my body assimilated the information, I now found that I also had a plan for doing groundwork with this supple and willing little horse for the next three months. I have had the pleasure of riding with many wonderful and insightful riding instructors, but I never expected that my next enlightenment would happen under the tutelage of a martial artist."

Rider Insight, Dian: "I have been taking lessons with James for almost three years. In that time, my entire concept of the art of riding has changed through the practice of Tai Chi. James shares with his students his teachings of inner balance and harmonies with the horse. He's taught me how to use my internal energy and economy of motion in relationship to my horse so that we truly move as one. It has been a joyful series of 'enlightenments' for me."

Rider Insight, Susan: "I met James at a national riding event in Columbus, Ohio. When I was told I'd be riding in two Tai Chi clinics, I wasn't sure what to expect. I had no previous knowledge of Tai Chi. After working with James for about fifteen minutes, I began to understand what he was trying to achieve. By the end of the second day I was amazed at the difference in my body. I was moving much better with Thor. I was able to sit his trot without my body and legs becoming stiff. My only regret is that we live on opposite sides of the country. I could really benefit from more instruction from James."

What Tai Chi Offers You

Incorporating Tai Chi into your riding and life offers you many rewards. As you pursue a softer, gentler approach to riding, you will:

- subtly change your position, creating a change in the horse
- soften your position for a truly independent seat, so your body and its movement will become relaxed and free of unnecessary tension
- feel yourself meld with your horse's rhythm

Tai Chi also helps you improve your general health. You will:
- increase your lung capacity
- stir your chi through your internal organs and enhance their functioning
- combat the effects of osteoporosis, as your bones direct the force of gravity in your body
- release stress down through your body to the ground, thus healing many stress-related diseases.

What's Next

In chapter 2, "Fundamentals of Tai Chi: An Ancient Art, A New Perspective," I will look at the principles underlying all the exercises ahead in the book. This will provide a basis for seeing the coherent system of knowledge that connects the many facets of Tai Chi.

Fundamentals of Tai Chi

An Ancient Art, A New Perspective

2

THIS CHAPTER INTRODUCES THE FUNDAMENTALS that underlie the exercises appearing later in the book. These fundamentals include Eight Principles that will guide our practice, as well as the "anatomy" of Tai Chi: the three Dain Tians, the fourteen meridians, and the Eight Gates, all of which direct how energy is held and moved throughout the body.

The Eight Principles

The training exercises and forms taught in this book are drawn from many different styles of internal arts, each emphasizing different motions and goals. Some are done for health and healing, others for meditation, and still others as a martial arts practice. The common thread that they all share is a set of underlying principles as described in the ancient Tai Chi classics, which describe each principle and teach its correct practice. Some of these principles translate into very clear and concise directions. Others are less direct, presenting concepts of one's relationship to nature, and they may seem esoteric if not vague. I suggest that if you seek the meanings of the latter with an open mind, you will discover ways in which they apply to riding.

I will do my best to relate each principle's meaning and application to riding. You also need to remember that any one person's experience and knowledge is limited—hence the saying, "Art is long, and life is short." With this in mind, please don't limit the meaning and application of these principles to your riding by your initial comprehension of their meaning. Your comprehension of them, like mine, will continue to grow throughout your practice.

1 Use the mind, not force

In all exercises, it is imperative that your mind directs all action. At no time do you want to fall victim to the unconscious actions of your body. If your mind does not direct the movement of your body, those movements will be rigid and out of rhythm. Inevitably this lack of rhythm leads to the use of force rather than sensitivity. Your conscious mind directs your *intent* (see p. 34), and your body follows. The body is limited by physics, but the mind can be developed infinitely beyond the limits of time and space.

2 Never oppose force with force

Tai Chi assumes a force bigger and stronger than you is trying to upset your balance—whether it be the conscious intent of an opponent or the unconscious action of your horse.

Whether mounted or on the ground, to confront the strength of a horse directly with your own strength is to lose. The result of this kind of battle can be seen in the bent and twisted body of many an old cowboy who spent decades opposing the force of horses. You will never be bigger or stronger than your horse. Using force is to lose not only the battle, but also the war.

3 Yield and overcome

Rather than oppose force with force, yield and overcome. This philosophy is best represented in an old Chinese story.

In a violent storm a mighty oak tree—tall, strong, and known its rigidity—stood against the mighty wind with all its strength. In the same storm a bamboo tree with its long and slender stalks was blown over to the ground as it yielded to the force of the storm. After the storm passed, the seemingly weak and fragile bamboo bounced back and once again reached to the sky. The majestic oak, which had tried to stand strong against the gale, lay uprooted with branches torn from its trunk.

4 Balance like a scale

When you practice, stand with your posture balanced like a scale. Your state of balance should be as sensitive as that of a scale, so that the slightest change of balance in either you or your horse will be detected. When you move, your movements should revolve effortlessly like turning a wheel.

Let your whole body move in harmony. As you compensate for the ever-changing balance of you and your horse, your movement should flow and circulate ceaselessly and without interruption.

Just as the movement of the wheel starts at the hub, so should all the movement of your body originate from your center. The slightest movement of your fingers in a rein aid should be connected to your center (seat). This principle involves a lifetime of thought and application.

5 Seek stillness in motion

This principle initially refers to maintaining a calm state of mind while your body is in motion, but as with all of our practice, it can lead to deeper and more profound experiences: "The water of the spring is clear, like crystal. The water of the pond is deep and placid. Your mind should be like that of the pond and your spirit like the spring."

I have experienced this feeling of stillness while riding when completely connected to my horse and we are moving together in one rhythmic flow, neither opposing nor resisting each other's force. I become aware of the sensation of being still while everything in my peripheral vision is moving. It's a calm and almost surrealistic feeling. It is much like standing in the middle of a moving carousel and perceiving that you are standing still while the world moves around you.

The ability to move all parts of your body as one coordinated unit is at the heart of this principle. You'll experience this state of stillness in motion and motion in stillness in the *Walking Backward* exercise in chapter 3 (see p. 62).

6 Be heavy and light

The root of heaviness is lightness. When you can be soft and pliable, and then, at will, hard and strong so that no force can upset your balance, you have mastered your internal energy, or chi.

Your mind controls and directs your chi, and chi can only flow through a calm and relaxed body. To achieve this, you must first calm and relax your breathing.

7 Focus and expand

Guard against developing tunnel vision, which leads to a narrowed view and decreased perceptivity. Remember that you want to increase your focus by expanding your awareness.

For example, if you are constantly looking down at your horse's head, you decrease your sensitivity to the rest of his body. Or, when riding on a circle, if you are not as aware of the center of the circle as you are the circumference on which you are trying to ride, it will be nearly impossible to ride a "perfect" circle. This does not mean that you must look in two directions at once, but rather that you should see the big picture.

8 Remember that art is long, life is short

More a philosophy than a principle, this saying reminds us that there is no end to learning the secrets of our art. My teacher after forty years of daily practice in Tai Chi once told me, "James, I still need to relax my fingers more." When I keep this in mind, it helps me to not become discouraged and frustrated when I have an off day or my discipline is less than I expect from myself.

Dain Tians

The *Dain Tians* are gathering places of energy and force within the body. You have three:

- The upper Dain Tian in the center of your head
- The middle Dain Tian at the center of your chest
- The lower Dain Tian behind your navel

When I refer to the Dain Tian and don't specify which one, I'm referring to the lower Dain Tian.

Visualize your lower Dain Tian as a gyroscope, encompassing 360 degrees of moving parts inside your body, including all the joints of your pelvis, and your lumbar and sacral spine.

Your Dain Tian is your center. *Every motion starts in your center.*

Meridians

Traditional Chinese medicine teaches that the body has fourteen meridians or channels:

- The Lung
- The Large Intestine
- The Stomach
- The Spleen
- The Heart
- The Small Intestine
- The Bladder
- The Kidney
- The Pericardium
- The Triple Warmer
- The Gall Bladder
- The Liver
- The Front and the Back Meridians (Rue and Due)

Visualize the area of the lower Dain Tian as if it were a gyroscope.

On all the meridians, there are a series of points. Each of these points can be manipulated to restrict or enhance the flow of chi through them. These are the points in which acupuncturists place needles or where acupressurists apply finger pressure to treat imbalances, ailments, or diseases. See the *Appendix*, p. 250, for a chart of the meridians.

Putting It All Together

Thus far we have discussed the *Eight Principles*, which describe a philosophy of employing chi for maximal benefit. We have also discussed the *Dain Tians* and *meridians*, which could be said to describe an "anatomy of chi," that is, the places in which chi gathers and the channels though which it moves. So, we have a spirit in which to work, and the energy and pathways with which to work. Now we need a system to control this energy. That control is provided by means of the *Eight Gates*. These gates control the rider's chi, and when the rider is well connected with the horse, the rider's gates also influence the horse's chi and movement.

The Eight Gates

The Eight Gates control the flow of the essential life force—chi—in the body. The gates are an integral part of the path we're traveling to develop our Tai Chi knowledge and skills, which we can then use to enhance our horsemanship. Each gate can be opened only with your mind, and opening the gates changes your body, changes your motion, and builds your awareness.

In addition to controlling the flow of your chi through the meridians within your body, the gates also affect the flow of chi between you and your horse. When all the gates are opened, the energy of you and your horse combine and are in harmony. When horse and rider are moving as one, energy is pumped through the Eight Gates, energizing your body as well as your horse's. As a pair you become one fluid energy, allowing for seamless transitions and nearly effortless aids.

When the gates are closed, they restrict or inhibit the synergistic flow of energy between horse and rider. When closed, the horse's energy is not allowed to flow through your body, so it effectively disconnects you from your horse.

By opening these gates, you will make subtle changes in your riding and increase the connection with your body and your horse. You'll use the gates in the exercises throughout the book.

Learning to open these gates on the ground is essential to opening them later while riding. The opening of a gate is a subtle relaxation and expansion of a particular area of your body. You open a gate first by visualization, which is then followed by directing and focusing your breath. While you are on the ground, the result of this opening is subtle; while riding, the result is profound.

Here are two stories that demonstrate what riders can achieve by opening their gates:

Rider Insight, Sue: While I was working with Sue, an advanced dressage rider, I coached her both on the ground and mounted to open Gate 7: The Upper Pass. The moment she opened this gate, her mare collected and softened to a level they had never achieved before. More important than the actual physical change in both was the deeper feeling of connection she felt with her horse.

Sue had owned this mare a long time, and always felt that somehow she was in the way of her own riding. She knew that her horse was capable of a higher level, but she just didn't know how to get it. For Sue, the lesson ended in tears of joy. She left with not only some new riding tools, but also a deeper bond with an old friend.

Rider Insight, Carrie: A young girl, Carrie, was ready to get rid of her horse because, even though she loved him, she could not control his energy and she felt that he was always running out from under her. (This was a gaited horse, very energetic and beautiful. With two big headstrong egos, they mirrored each other perfectly.) We worked together for two days to open her Gate 2: the Ming Meng, and Gates 3 and 4: the Front and Back of the Heart gates. As the gates opened, more of the horse's energy came up into Carrie, enabling her to join with and control the energy of her horse without having to "squish" it down.

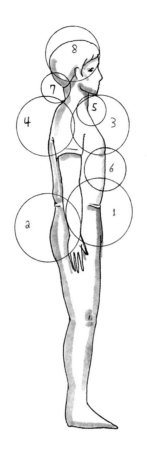

The Eight Gates

1 The Dain Tian (lower)

2 The Ming Meng

3 The Front of the Heart

4 The Back of the Heart

5 The Chi Who (right and left)

6 The Liver and Spleen

7 The Upper Pass
   (at the base of the skull)

8 The Crown

Again the greatest effect of the opening of these gates was the release of emotional frustration that Carrie felt toward her horse—and the fact that he was no longer for sale.

Opening the Eight Gates

This section lists the gates and the effects of each gate being either opened or closed. While there are tangible physical motions that precede the opening of all the gates, these motions alone are not enough. Your mind must first direct that the gate open; only then can the physical change in your body actually open the gate. Remember that in Tai Chi there are no limits to the development of the mind. The only limits are the ones that we place on ourselves. (See *Appendix*, p. 245, for diagrams of human skeletal and muscular anatomy.)

Gate 1: The Dain Tian

Where: As I mentioned, there are three major Dain Tians (gathering places of energy) in Chinese medicine. We will concentrate on the lower in this book. The lower Dain Tian is located inside the body approximately 2 inches below the navel. The lower Dain Tian is also known as the "chi bank," because it is believed to be the area in which the chi resides.

Opened: When opened, this gate allows your breath to drop into your abdomen, effectively lowering your center of gravity. It relaxes your hips and abdomen, creating a deeper, more solid seat. With practice you can use the opening and closing of Gate 1 to initiate a halt or walk.

Closed: Riding with the Dain Tian closed inhibits your breathing and creates tension in your waist and hips. This tightness leads to your feeling of riding *on* the horse, not *with* the horse. When the rider's Dain Tian opens, the horse's topline immediately softens and he relaxes. The strides become lighter and the head lowers.

The abdominal breathing techniques in the following chapters are the initial key to opening the lower Dain Tian.

Exercises used to facilitate the opening of the Dain Tian: *Heaven and Earth* (p. 106), *Counting Your Breath* (p. 97), and *Wall Sitting* (p. 59).

Gate 2: The Ming Meng

Where: The Ming Meng is located on your spine in your lower back, directly behind the navel. *Gate 2: The Ming Meng* is also referred to as the "gate of life" because it is the first gate to be energized and is the gate where chi flows into and up the spinal cord.

Opened: Opening Gate 2: The Ming Meng allows for a further expansion of your lower back and deepening of your breath. This gate's opening enables your lower lumbar region to move more freely, thus deepening the seat. When your lower body is relaxed and centered, the balance of your upper body is easier to maintain. The muscles of your upper back and chest can relax and therefore allow for the opening of the heart gates.

Opening the Ming Meng creates more "throughness" in the horse by engaging the hind end while lightening the forehand. Your new balance means the horse does not have to divide his energy and focus between balancing you and moving freely forward. Opening the Ming Meng puts the rider's center deep into the pelvis (rather than up in the chest). Only if the center is in the Ming Meng can the rider be in self-carriage, and until the rider is in self-carriage, the horse cannot be in self-carriage.

Closed: If you keep the Ming Meng closed while riding, you experience tightening of the lower back and restriction of breath. In the horse, it restricts the motion of the hind end and leads to tightness in the withers.

Exercises used to facilitate the opening of the Ming Meng are: *Horse Stance and Wall Sitting* (p. 56), *Walking Backward* (p. 62), *Heaven and Earth* (p. 106), and *Open the Ming Meng* (p. 99).

Gate 3: The Front of the Heart

Opened: Opening *Gate 3: The Front of the Heart* helps relax your chest and lower your shoulders, and so keeps your elbows down. This, in turn, quiets your hands. You will feel more of your horse, because the energy can move up through your Ming Meng and Dain Tian into your heart and upper body, out through your arms to your hands, and back into the horse via the reins. This is *connection.* It is impossible to ride with your front heart gate open and carry negative thoughts or emotions. Negative states directly affect your horse's trust in you and his willingness to collect.

> *Rider Insight, Sue: "When my front heart gate opened, I suddenly realized that my energy and motion moving up from my lower body was for the first time no longer hitting a 'wall' at the level of my heart. Suddenly my horse and I became one single energy unit. It was no longer my smaller mass riding my horse's larger*

mass—his 1200 pounds and my 140. My entire sense of mass disappeared, and I could lift his back with my intent and creativity rather than with effort and work."

I believe in a higher level of communication between horse and rider than merely the physical act of riding. When connected, the horse will follow your intent. Your intent is created in your mind and projected through your heart when your front heart gate is open. *Only through an open heart can you communicate your intent to your horse.*

Exercises to facilitate opening the heart: *Heaven and Earth* (p. 62), *Spread Your Chest* (p. 126), *Spread Your Wings* (p. 131), and *Bend with an Arch* (p. 154).

Gate 4: The Back of the Heart

Opened: Opening *Gate 4: The Back of the Heart* further relaxes your upper back and neck muscles. This relaxation allows your thoracic and cervical vertebrae to move more freely with the rhythm of the horse. Opening the Back of the Heart also lengthens the reach of your arms, so that your elbows can stay bent and pointing down without pulling on the reins. This position allows your shoulders, elbows, wrists, and fingers to act as shock absorbers between the horse's mouth and the movements in your body.

> *Rider Insight, Trish:* "Thank you for the awesome experience I had during your clinic. The breakthroughs I had affected not only my work with horses but other areas of my life as well. You were so right in your assessment of me being a very closed person. I don't allow very much to come into me, so asking me to open my heart was huge for me. Opening from the back has made it all possible.
>
> "Since the clinic I have found I react differently when Nick, my very sensitive Thoroughbred, spooks. I am quieter, calmer, and can focus through the upset and go back to work faster. I have also noticed a change in his attitude toward me. He seems to be easier to get along with on the ground. Maybe that is just my change in (heart) attitude toward him. I'm learning to trust on a deeper level."

Closed: When the Back of your Heart is closed, your muscles are holding your upper spine in place and resisting the motion of the horse to maintain balance. This is often the root cause of shoulder tension and tightness in the neck. You transfer this tightness through your arms and hands to the horse. Your horse reflects the tightness through stiffness in his neck and chest.

When you ride with your heart closed (left), the reins function like ropes tied high in a tree: they have great leverage, and using this advantage, your horse can easily uproot your seat. Opening the Back of the Heart (right) is like moving the rope down to the trunk of the tree: the leverage is decreased and your seat is strong and rooted.

The reason so many riders keep the Back of the Heart closed is that the tension created acts as an anchor or brace for the arms and hands to pull from. This anchor leads to a false sense of centered strength that becomes apparent when the rider is pulled forward out of her seat by a small tug of the horse's head.

Holding in the upper back (heart gate closed) causes you to use your trapezius and rhomboid muscles to maintain balance. It leads to a disconnection between your upper body and seat.

Riding with a closed heart restricts the ability of your chest and abdomen to expand during inhalation, inhibiting your body's rhythm. Opening the Back of the Heart causes your latissimus dorsi muscles to engage. In doing so, you're physically connecting the reins to your seat through your bones and muscles.

Riding with an open heart releases tension in the horse's neck and shoulders. It allows for more complete collection and opens the path for communicating thought and intent.

The back's larger muscles and their attachments to the spine, shoulder, and upper arm (humerus), properly used in relaxation (left), and improperly used (right)—note the raised shoulder and jutting elbow.

Exercises to facilitate opening Gate 4: The Back of the Heart: *Wall Sitting* (p. 59), and *Embracing the Moon* (p. 102).

Gate 5: The Chi Who (Right and Left)

Where: Gate 5: The Chi Who (right and left sides) are located just below the collarbones in line between the nipples and ear lobes. To locate one, hold your arm out to your side at shoulder level, and form an "OK" sign with your index finger and thumb. Bend your arm at the elbow until your hand touches your chest. The center of the circle created by your fingers marks the location of the Chi Who (see photo).

Opened: Opening the Chi Who gates directly affects the softness and sensitivity of your hands to the bit. It plays a major role in stabiliz-

The location of the Chi Who gate, just below the collarbone.

ing the upper body during trot and canter. Opening the Chi Who relaxes and releases tension in the muscles of the chest and neck, allowing the head to move in rhythm with the rest of your body and the horse. When your trapezius, deltoids, and pectoral muscles are relaxed and your latissimus dorsi muscles are engaged, you allow your shoulders to move independently of your spine (see *Appendix,* p. 245, for anatomy chart). Your shoulders act as shock absorbers between your torso and the horse's mouth.

If you observe very advanced riders from behind, it looks as though their spine is moving up and down with the rise and fall of the horse's body, but the shoulders remain at relatively the same level as the spine moves

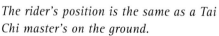
The rider's position is the same as a Tai Chi master's on the ground.

between them. I first observed this independence in the German dressage rider Klaus Balkenhol during the 1996 Olympics in Atlanta. His position on the horse was the same as a Tai Chi master's would be on the ground (see drawings).

With Gate 5: the Chi Who open, it is impossible to use the front of your chest to brace against the horse's pulling on the reins. If you do brace—thereby closing the Chi Who—you may find yourself being jerked out of the saddle by the horse, which disconnects the two of you. You'd also allow the horse to halt or fall out of his gait.

Looking at the same scenario—this time with an open Chi Who—when the horse pulls on the reins, the force travels up through the bones of your arms. As the force travels up your arms, it is transferred into the latissimus dorsi muscles, which then take the force down to the lower half of your back and seat. The force effectively pulls you deeper into your mount. If, in the moment that the horse pulls against the reins, you tighten the muscles of your chest and shoulders, the force is transferred through the shoulders to the upper back and neck via the trapezius muscles. It is then a matter of relative strength; the horse, being bigger and stronger, always wins this tug-o-war.

Closed: With the Chi Who closed, you will rely on the muscles of your upper body to hold yourself in balance. This is not a particular problem at the walk. However, as soon as the motion becomes bigger, your muscles have to work harder to hold your mass over your now moving center (seat). Soon your shoulders come up, your elbows go out, and your abdomen tightens. This all happens unconsciously as your body goes into self-preservation mode in an attempt to literally *hold itself* in balance.

I see these symptoms in many beginning and intermediate riders. This is not to say that all, or even most, advanced riders open their Chi Who, but they just become better at hiding the effects of riding with it closed. In advanced riders, the signs of a closed Chi Who are seen as tightness in the muscles of the jaw and the front of the neck. This tightness is the result of having to *hold* the head balanced over the upper body much in the same way the beginner holds her upper body over her center.

I suggest two ways of relaxing the jaw and neck. The first approach you can try is to smile, but if the Chi Who is closed, the smiling will not last and soon your neck and jaw will tighten again. The second, deeper approach, opening *Gate 7: The Upper Pass* and *Gate 8: The Crown* is addressed a little later in this section.

A closed Gate 6: The Liver and Spleen (left) and the soft and yielding abdomen of an open Gate 6 (right).

Opening the Upper Pass and the Crown gates helps you maintain your head and neck in a relaxed and aligned position that helps, in turn, to keep the Chi Who open. All gates are integrated, part of a path, and thus action on one affects the others.

Exercises to facilitate opening Gate 5: The Chi Who: *Neck Turns* (p. 121), *Spread Your Chest* (p. 126), and *Spread Your Wings* (p. 131).

Gate 6: The Liver and Spleen

Where: The Liver and Spleen gates are located, as you'd guess, near the liver (right side) and spleen (left side)—that is, just below the rib cage in line with the nipples. While these are two, separate gates, I'm counting them as one for these reasons:

1 They are both opened in the same way. In fact, it is nearly impossible to open one and not the other.

2 They are mirror images of each other, and the left and right serve the same function, namely, transferring energy back to the horse laterally.

These two gates should be the last two you try to open, as inexperience keeping the other gates open while focusing on these will often shut all of your gates.

Opened: The opening of Gate 6: The Liver and Spleen creates an incredible connection between you and your horse during lateral work. When open, these gates allow the horse's energy to move from the horse's hindquarters through your abdomen, with no restriction or blocks, into your hand. To open these gates, you must first be able to relax your abdomen completely as you'll learn in the abdominal breathing exercises in chapter 4. You can then use your intent to soften and expand the gate while inhaling in order to ensure that this region of your abdomen is completely relaxed.

Often, when I watch a rider performing lateral work, such as half-pass or shoulder-in, I see a great deal of resistance in the abdomen just below the rib cage. This resistance arises when the horse's body moves forward and to the side, and the rider's center moves out of rhythm with her upper body. Unconsciously, she tightens the abdomen and her upper body gets pulled along with the center. Remember, all this happens without a thought and in a fraction of a second, but that is enough to break the rhythm and upset the combined balance of horse and rider.

With The Liver and Spleen gates opened, they act to make your center bigger and more sensitive while creating a true connection between your seat and upper body. When I ride, it feels as if the horse's energy or force moves first through the open gate a moment prior to my seat and abdomen moving. Energetically, it is as if the horse leads the gate, and the gate leads the body. Physically, it feels like riding a wave that starts in the horse. Let's say the right hind moves through my right seat bone and hip—it's then transferred diagonally through the abdomen and out the spleen (left) gate.

Exercises to facilitate opening Gate 6: The Liver and Spleen: *Hold the Sky with Both Hands* (p. 138), and *Thrust Palm in Bow Stance* (p. 146).

Gate 7: The Upper Pass

Where: Gate 7: The Upper Pass is located at the base of the skull, where the head and spine come together, and is where the chi passes from the lower body into the head.

Opened: When the Upper Pass gate is opened, your mind is clear and focused, and you ride with a heightened sense of awareness.

There are more than seven muscles that either attach or pass through the Upper Pass. When you use the outermost of these muscles to hold your head in balance, the pass is closed and tension is present. Opening the Upper Pass engages the innermost muscles to connect your head and spine. These muscles are smaller postural muscles that by design were meant to hold up the bones against gravity. They can be engaged without hindering the motion and rhythm of the head, neck, and spine. Therefore, they allow your head to stay balanced and the outermost muscles to remain soft and sensitive. The bigger and more open the Upper Pass, the easier it is to balance the head without using the larger muscles of your neck, shoulders, and upper back.

The energy that empowers your intent comes through the Upper Pass. With your skull and neck in the proper position, you open the Upper Pass with your mind or your intent. I visualize it opening like a shutter of a camera—it spirals open.

My Riding Insight: While working with a dressage competitor, I noticed that her whole body looked relaxed except for her jaw and neck. This made it very difficult for her to smile while riding. I knew that she was not making a conscious choice not to smile, but nevertheless, soon after I would remind her to smile, it would disappear. Knowing that the tension in the muscles of her neck, face, and upper back was there to hold her head in balance, we looked for another way to keep her head balanced and in rhythm with the rest of her body and her horse.

I remembered that in my own riding, when I opened my Upper Pass and expanded my Crown my head felt light and floating (not light-headed, but physically light) I took a moment to explain the idea of opening the Upper Pass and Crown, and then we gave it a try in the saddle. After a few moments of moving her awareness to the Upper Pass, it opened. Immediately her neck and jaw softened, her shoulders dropped slightly, and the smile on her face was beautiful and effortless. What I did not expect was that the sound of the horse's hooves hitting the ground became very soft, and he seemed to get bigger and rounder.

Exercises to facilitate opening Gate 7: The Upper Pass: *Walking Backward* (p. 62), and *Neck Turns* (p. 121).

Gate 8: The Crown

Where: *Gate 8: The Crown* is located at the top of your head. Think of where a crown would sit; the Crown gate is the entire area that a crown would cover. The opening of this gate is often associated with enlightenment. Creativity—your seventh sense—enters through the Crown gate. In Eastern healing arts this area is referred to as the Crown chakra.

Opened: The Crown gate is opened primarily with your intent. That is, you consciously focus your intent on the area and see it opening. Visualize it opening like the petals of a flower opening with the morning sun.

Opening this gate is said to increase your conscious contact with the divine. My own experience is that when I open my Crown, I always feel a chill of energy run down and then up my spine. It is usually such a strong sensation that it makes me shiver for a moment.

As with all the Eight Gates, it is not enough to merely "think" the gate open. Your intent must be supported by the proper position of your body. For your Crown to open you must "suspend the top of your head"—aligning your head and center with the heavens above. Classical Tai Chi asserts that suspending of the head has the effect of promoting one's spirit and preventing one from being heavy and clumsy.

To suspend the head correctly, keep your chin slightly inward and straighten your neck. Your eyes gaze slightly below the horizon—lowered approximately 25 degrees, which, when mounted means that you look ahead between the horse's ears. In this traditional riding posture, your head is lifted as if it were suspended from the heavens by a thread.

Position your head by sensing—not by using force—and avoid any muscle tension in your neck. This position must be maintained regardless of the movement of the rest of your body. When your crown is suspended, it acts to lift your head in such a way as to bring your chin down lightly and lift the head from the vertebrae in the neck. In short, it balances your head on your spine. I've noticed that riders at the higher levels, often on big, strong, and highly energetic horses, tend to hold the head in balance with the muscles in the neck, which creates tension in the jaw and front of the neck.

A dressage competitor that I was working with learned to remove the tension in her face and neck simply by suspending her head and smiling. The impact on her horse was amazing, as he gave his back completely and seemed to float through his strides.

Exercises to facilitate opening Gate 8: The Crown: *Standing Meditation* (p. 37), *Walking Backward* (p. 62), *Neck Turns* (p. 121), and *Lift a Single Iron Arm* (p. 158).

What's Next

In the next chapter, "Your Mind: Awakening Self-Awareness and the Creative Mind," we will begin to lay the foundation of all the work to come by exploring awareness and the mind-body connection that is essential to enhancing *everything* we do, both on and off the horse.

Your Mind

3

Awakening Self-Awareness and the Creative Mind

I N THIS CHAPTER, YOU WILL DISCOVER a deeper level of awareness of your body that precedes the mind-body connection. You will experience being in a truly balanced state, both mind *and* body. You will see how small changes in your body's alignment and movement can create huge differences in your ability to relax and stay balanced. This makes your horse's job of supporting you much easier. This first series of exercises, based on traditional Tai Chi forms, offers you a simple way to expand your awareness and help develop your mind-body connection.

Unified Learning

To begin any new endeavor without first unifying mind and body by becoming aware of your physical state is at best inefficient. Self-awareness is the first step toward unifying your mind and body. Without self-awareness, you will be trapped in your old ways of thinking and moving. Realize that out of a twenty-four-hour day, you may ride for two hours, sleep for eight, and the other fourteen you're in old habits. The exercises will help you identify your own habits of imbalance on the ground, where they are more easily discovered. At the same time, the exercises will teach you a new and more balanced way to move. Remember that bad habits don't just go away—they must be deliberately replaced.

> "We must go beyond thought, go beyond visualization, go beyond imagination, and actually open a part of the mind that is usually closed and untapped in most people."
>
> (Deng Ming-Dao, from *365 Tao Daily Meditations*)

To build your awareness, you will explore the relationship between balance and tension, gravity and structural alignment, breath and intent. During these exercises, you will be asked to reflect back to the principles from chapter 2, and apply your knowledge of them to enhance your experience and understanding of your body in stillness and in motion. You will become aware of your strengths. You will learn more effectively on the ground, so all the exercises start with ground work. The knowledge you gain you'll later apply directly to your riding and your relationship to your horse.

Permission to Learn

Have you ever watched a young child who is learning to walk? Her parents step back and encourage her to come toward them. Her intent is to move forward, even if her legs are unsure. She staggers forward following her intent. Without being taught, she has taken her first steps. When she develops her motor skills, she never has to think about walking. It just happens, with or without her awareness. In a sense we first learn to walk by stumbling. When it's time to learn something new, do you still give yourself permission to stumble?

Sensing and Intent

One of the most powerful and often misunderstood tools available to you while riding is your *intent*. Intent is a *stretching of your mind toward a certain goal or object*. Proper use of your intent allows you to see and prepare for changes prior to the actual change. Whether the change is in the horse's gait or asking for collection, your intent projects what you envision or create in your mind.

Here's a story that demonstrates the power of intent. Once, while working with a dressage trainer on a young horse, I asked her to extend her trot as she reached a pre-arranged spot in the arena. While she approached the mark, I watched as she asked for extension. Within three strides she achieved an extended trot, and we thought, "Pretty good for a young horse." I then asked her what her focus was prior to giving the aid. She said that she was paying close attention to the horse in anticipation of the correct time to give the aid for extended trot. Reminding me of her horse's youth, she added that he rarely, if ever, responded to her aids in the moment she applied them.

Prior to her second attempt, I asked her do two things: (1) to see the extension of the trot in her mind's eye long before the two reached their spot, and (2) rather than focus on her horse as she gave the aids, to focus her intent on being light and balanced in the saddle. Now the two achieved the desired trot within one stride. On their next pass, their trot extended the moment they passed through the desired spot. The difference was that her intent was clear and in the right place prior to giving the physical aids. Because the rider focused on her own body position and balance, her horse could do the same.

Consider the horse's experience of this same situation: have you ever tried to complete a task with someone breathing down your neck, ready to correct any mistake you might make? It's nerve-racking to say the least, and it's not a situation apt to help you perform at your best. I believe that when the rider above used her intent to create a clear picture of the desired trot in her mind prior to asking for it, the horse was able to understand the goal without any physical communication.

A gifted equine dentist once told me that the moment he sets foot on a property, every horse there can sense any fear, anger, frustration, or anxiety he has held in his body. Before any horse allows him to do his work, he must remove those emotions. By the way, he performs all his work without the use of drugs to numb his patients, and they relax and melt into him with complete trust as he is working. It seems that even if you are unaware of it, your intent is at work. You'll explore and experience intent through the *Walking Backward* exercise later in this chapter.

With the understanding that your intent is constantly at work, it is of vital importance to know what you are projecting. Rather than trying to identify many so-called "negative" emotions that may show up with you at the barn on any given day, you will let them go and replace them by focusing on the body. A quiet, calm mind is the only place to develop and explore this tool.

Your mind's eye—also called the third eye or your "inner" eye—is a versatile tool in riding. When you open your mind's eye, you can progress from being a good rider, who's wise in the techniques of horsemanship, to being an enlightened equestrian. You'll employ this sense—this "knowing" yourself and your horse as one—whenever you handle your horse on the ground or ride him. Chapter 6 further develops heightening this sense.

Safety

In each exercise, remember to follow safety procedures. Choose an open area, without any hazards or obstacles like jumps or cavaletti. In the saddle, have a friend assist you, possibly by holding the horse while he's standing still, and certainly to longe you in a corral or round pen. If you're riding in an enclosed area and you know your horse well, you can ride with the reins dropped.

The First and Only Rule: Smile and Breathe!

This is the book's only rule, and it applies to all the exercises. Smile and breathe—it's good to be alive! Riding is fun. Tai Chi will enhance the pleasures you share with your horse.

And here's another reason for smiling: you relax and soften. Look at a young rider—when her pony misbehaves, she laughs and relaxes. When you're relaxed and your horse rears or spooks, think of what happens: instead of tensing—which communicates more anxiety to your horse—your body softens. You reconnect with your horse to counteract the rearing or spooking.

So, smile and breathe. Practice seriously—but don't be too serious when you practice!

Standing Meditation

Riding Goal: Balance

Your goals are to develop a new awareness and understanding of balance in *Standing Meditation* on the ground. Later you will carry this learning with you onto the horse, where you will experience and develop a state of quiet stillness in the saddle, which I call *Sitting Meditation*. This exercise teaches you the different roles the bones, muscles, and mind play in maintaining your balance.

Function

This exercise has three important functions: it introduces and teaches you to achieve true balance; it defines the roles of your muscles and bones in maintaining balance; and it leads to discovery of your body's inherent strengths and weaknesses.

Intent

You'll use your mind to observe the changes in your body as you alter your alignment. This exercise is the first step to learning how to listen to your body. In classic Tai Chi forms this situation is known as *wu ji* or "double-weighted." This is the only time in a Tai Chi form that your weight remains distributed 50/50 in both feet. At all other times you pass through 50/50 weight distribution as you move from one position to the next. During this exercise you feel what it is like to move your body with your mind. This will be your introduction to the principle of using your mind, not force.

Step-by-Step

1 Stand in a shoulder-width parallel stance. Your legs are straight, neither locked nor bent. Your knees are relaxed. Your arms hang naturally at your sides, with the hands relaxed.

Stand with your feet parallel to each other, that is, they point directly forward and are neither pigeon-toed nor splayed.

Here's how to check that your feet are shoulder-width: keeping the ball of your left foot in place, swing your left heel 90 degrees toward the toes of your right foot. When your left foot is perpendicular to the right, you should see a space of one fist between the heel of your left foot and the toes of your right.

James On Your Shoulder

Smiling is the best way to relax over 100 muscles in and around your face. Also, it's very hard to hold on to negative thoughts while smiling. I believe that a horse is well aware of your mental state, and a negative mind will not achieve positive results. Have you ever had to spend a long period of time around negative people? How did it feel? If you had a choice, would you stay in their company? Would you feel connected with them? Your horse would give, I believe, similar answers.

Steps 1 and 2

Steps 4 and 6: If your weight is in your heels (left) allow it to move to the balls of your feet (right).

2 Look forward to the horizon. Smile and breathe.

3 Next, suspend your head as if it were held from above by a silken thread, or you can imagine the crown of your head floating upward. This idea and visualization acts to put your head and neck in proper alignment, without creating undue tension in the muscles of your neck.

Try to imagine that you are just a skeleton with no muscles to hold up your bones. How would you have to align your bones to keep them standing?

4 Now become aware of where your weight is in your feet. How is that weight distributed? Equally between the two feet, or more in one foot or the other? Evenly within your feet, or with more weight to the inside or outside? More weight in your heels, or more weight in the balls of your feet? Make a mental note of what you find because this has an important connection to your riding: where your weight is in your feet on the ground tells you where your weight is in your seat in the saddle. We'll return to this in the mounted portion of this exercise. For now, simply focus your mind on the balls of your feet. Put 100 percent of your focus and concentration there.

Most people stand with their weight back in the heel of the foot (see photo). In that position, you lack structural alignment and you have less strength. When you stand with your weight in your heels, you are at the "end of your rope" as far as balance is concerned. Why? Because the slightest push on your chest will send you backward out of balance with very little chance to recover.

5 Now move your attention to your breathing. Take two or three deep, slow breaths, and with every breath relax a little more.

6 Become aware of your body, and check your weight: has it shifted into the balls of your feet? If your weight is still in your heels, allow it to move into the balls of your feet.

Next, we will adapt the work we've been doing on the ground to being on the horse.

Exploring Weight, Balance, and Strength

Try this test with a friend. Stand with your weight back in your heels. Have a friend push gently on your chest with one hand as if to push you backward (top photo).

Notice how you react. Do you tense your muscles in an attempt to hold your position? Do you push your hips forward toward your friend? Do you hold your breath? Do your arms or elbows come up? Does your chin drop and your eyes look down? Before you fall will you grab onto your friend's arms?

In the saddle, your horse serves as your friend. When you begin to lose your alignment, all these same things are likely to happen. They are *symptoms* of imbalance, not *causes*.

Now stand with your weight in the balls of your feet and relax all your muscles. Have your friend slowly push again (bottom photo).

Notice how much more strength you have to resist the push. Can you relax your muscles, especially your gluteals and quadriceps? Can you continue breathing? While your friend pushes, can you drop more weight into your feet? The point of this practice is not that you won't be pushed over; the point is that when you are properly aligned, maintaining your balance is much easier, even when your body is being moved by an outside force.

There are two principles behind allowing your weight to move: (1) all motion is directed by your mind; and (2) your body will seek perfect balance on its own *if you relax*. When the weight drops through your bones into the balls of your feet, you are in true structural alignment. You are balanced. In this position, listen to your body. Do you sense any tension you can now release? When your body is not in structural alignment, your muscles must hold a certain amount of tension to support the misalignment, often resulting in an assortment of predispositions for strains and injuries. After achieving proper alignment, the muscle may still hold this tension as a result of training or habit. Structurally aligned bones will allow you to let go of the tension in your muscles. In return, you will feel stronger and more grounded in this stance.

Sitting Meditation

If you have not just done *Standing Meditation*, return to the beginning of that exercise (p. 37) and tune yourself into the quiet, relaxed, strong, and balanced state that you can achieve. When done, keep that feeling in mind, and then begin *Sitting Meditation*.

Step-by-Step

1 Mount your horse and remain at the halt.

2 Look forward to the horizon. Smile and breathe.

3 Expand your crown upward. Visualize your head lifting, so you feel like you're floating upward. Feel the lift through all of your vertebrae, not just the top of your spine. That is, feel that the floating comes from expanding the small space between every vertebra in your spine, not from trying to stretch your neck up.

4 Relaxed and focused in the saddle, now become aware of where your weight is in your seat bones. Focus your mind on these bones. Try to feel what I call the "bone-to-leather connection." Put 100 percent of your focus and concentration there.

5 Earlier, I said that where your weight is in your feet mirrors where your weight is in your seat bones. Is this true for you? Where is your weight in your seat bones?

Just as most people stand with their weight back in their heels, most riders place their weight back in their seat bones. And just as when most people shift their weight forward to the balls of their feet they initially report that they feel as if they're leaning forward, most riders, when they move their weight to the center of their seat bones, report that they're leaning forward. While this impression is entirely normal, it's also inaccurate: you've actually found your center. With time, this position will feel "normal"—not to mention stronger, more supple, and better connected with your horse.

6 Again, focus on your "bone-to-leather" connection. Visualize your seat bones. How big are they? As big as golf balls? Tennis balls? See them and feel them. Where is your weight in that sphere you are envisioning?

7 Now move your attention to your breathing. Take two or three deep, slow breaths, and with every breath relax a little more.

8 Smile and sit quietly on your horse. Appreciate the relaxed, deep balanced seat you have right now. Your goal is to have this seat whenever you ride.

Ah-Ha!

When you are in *Standing Meditation*, with your bones aligned to support your body against gravity, you will feel heavier. As we have discussed, when you first experience being in true alignment, you may feel as if you are leaning forward, a sensation that will go away with time, as you get used to your new balance. Most of us have been living behind our center for all of our adult life, and we've become comfortable with and accustomed to our imbalance.

Here's a little test you can easily do to check your alignment. While in *Standing Meditation*, have a friend push straight down on your shoulders. You should feel the added force drop though your body into the ground, without having to tense or resist the force. If you are not in alignment, you will tighten the muscles of your abdomen, making it harder to breathe. At the same time, your hips will push forward to negotiate the added load, and the muscles of your lower back will tighten to compensate for the misalignment of your spine. Your body will respond in the same way when riding as your horse moves and gravity pushes down on you—unless you are properly aligned to negotiate the force.

Ability Transition

Throughout your day, you will begin to catch yourself with your weight in your heels. Weight in your heels will start to feel unbalanced. You will also notice that when your weight is centered, you need to use your muscles less to hold your body upright. You will start to hear your body like never before. You will recognize when you are overusing your muscles to compensate for misalignment. Remember that over your lifetime, you have trained your muscles to compensate for your structural misalignment.

Reminder

This exercise is used primarily to build your awareness of balance and how a lack of balance creates tension in your body. You have begun to develop the roadmap to a place of quiet connection with your horse. You have embarked upon a path, which is a pattern of initiating movement by using your mind, breath, and body.

In a Tai Chi form, the only time your weight is distributed 50/50 between your two feet is at the beginning and the end of the form. The same should be true for your riding. Your weight is only 50/50 in your seat bones when your horse is standing still and square. At any other moment, your weight is in transition. Balance in riding is not static, but dynamic and ever-shifting. The weight in your seat bones passes through this 50/50 point, but is never held or caught there. Whether in Tai Chi or riding, your goal is fluidity.

Side Step

Riding Goal: Balance

You will learn how to shift your weight effectively from one seat bone to another without negatively affecting your center and balance. You will ride more effectively by doing less.

Function

Side Step increases your ability to use your pelvis to negotiate your balance between the top and bottom of your body. This ability relieves tension in your lower back and teaches you to move your body as one whole unit. You'll develop a new understanding of your body alignment and balance.

This exercise builds on the awareness you experienced in *Standing Meditation.* You'll discover how you compensate for lack of structural alignment and how this compensation may interfere with your communication with the horse.

Intent

Imagine that the ball of your foot is a stake driven deep into the ground. That stake is the root of your balance while shifting your weight. Focus deep into your pelvis. Only then can you begin to move muscles consciously that up until now have only worked unconsciously.

Step-by-Step

1 Begin in *Standing Meditation.*

2 Now move your two feet slightly closer together, in preparation for the next step.

3 Step out to the side into a shoulder-width parallel stance without leaning to one side. You'll step and then shift your weight from one foot to the other. Move your left or right foot out into the shoulder-width parallel stance, without looking down. Ask yourself if your feet are parallel and a shoulder-width apart. What is the answer?

4 Now look down and compare the positions of your feet with where you thought they would be. If your feet aren't placed where you expected, reposition them to the correct position. Take a moment to experience what that position feels like.

Sometimes we think we know where our body is, but upon honest investigation we find it's not where we thought it was. For example, many times while working with a rider at the rising trot, I'll ask her if she thinks she is straight during the brief sitting phase. Most often she says, "Yes." When I tell her that actually she's leaning forward, she usually doesn't believe it. I must then employ onlookers to help me convince her that what she thinks is straight is not. As we continue to work and she is finally able to sit straight, she says that she feels as if she is leaning backward. It takes time and help to overcome this false knowing. A videotape is very helpful in this situation and can save a great deal of time and frustration.

5 Step back into the beginning position (with your feet closer together).

6 Step out once again into a shoulder-width stance. This time notice if you must lean to one side to take the step.

Of the riders I have worked with, I would say that 99 percent must lean to move one foot. This may not seem like a big deal in riding, but remember that how you have trained yourself to move on the ground is how you move in the saddle.

If you have to lean to pick up and reposition your foot—in other words to shift your weight—then you will do the same thing to some extent when you shift your weight from one seat bone to another. Most riders are unaware of this lean in the saddle, but I assure you that your horse is not.

To shift your weight without leaning, you must use your pelvis. *Side Step* helps you learn to move your pelvis directly, rather than first tensing it and your (stationary) supporting leg and then moving your center over the tensed leg by leaning in order to lighten the foot you want to lift.

7 Try this: take a deep breath and relax your abdomen. Imagine all your weight pouring like sand into the ball of your right foot. With this clearly in your mind, stretch your tailbone down as if there were a large, heavy weight attached to it. This is known as "dropping the tailbone." Note this is not tucking the tailbone under or pushing it forward as in a pelvic thrust.

Step 2   Step 3   Step 5   Step 6

8 As your tailbone drops, bend your left leg slightly at the knee and feel your leg becoming lighter and lighter. When 100 percent of your weight has shifted from your left leg into your right—no sooner—you may step out to the side.

This shift may seem like a very simple task, but there is a wealth of knowledge contained in this very unassuming exercise. The movement in the pelvis necessary to step out without leaning is the same movement used in a sitting trot to follow the motion of your horse. To develop this conscious movement is the difference between a good sitting trot and a great sitting trot.

Step 7   Step 8

Ah-Ha!

You will start to feel your weight shift inside your body before you perform any outside movement. You're engaging yourself, just as your horse engages his hindquarters. You will become increasingly aware of smaller and smaller percentages of weight shift. As you step, you will feel as if you are growing taller, or the crown of your head is stretching upward.

Ability Transition

Throughout your day you will increasingly catch yourself whenever you slip back into your old habit of leaning with your spine to initiate movement—rather than engaging your pelvis and moving from your center. Stop, pause, take a deep breath, and then move correctly—from your center.

In the saddle, you will be able to shift your weight and negotiate the movement of your horse through your body more efficiently and with less effort.

Reminder

Take your time and really listen to your body. Look for tension and unnecessary contractions of your muscles. Use your breath to help relax your body and let go of tension.

Wrist Shaking

Riding Goals: Balance, Relaxation, Body Control

You will gain a new awareness of your balance and what your horse may feel when compensating for your lack of balance. You will learn to stay relaxed in mind and body while riding. This relaxation in turn allows the horse to move more freely without constantly having to adjust for your imbalance. This freer movement increases both horse and rider endurance, because both of you are using less muscle to achieve greater results.

Function

The exercise develops a new understanding of body alignment and balance. When done properly, this exercise helps you to use and move your body as a coherent whole. You experience bouncing that helps relax and warm up all the joints and connective tissues of your body. This exercise helps you understand how body, mind, and breath can be used to refine balance and relaxation. Also, it teaches how a slight imbalance in your body leads to unnecessary fatigue and tension.

Intent

During *Wrist Shaking*, use your mind primarily to monitor muscle tension and breathing. However, this exercise requires your mind to stay calm and attentive to the smallest of changes in your body. Practice *Wrist Shaking* after learning *Standing Meditation*.

Step-by-Step

As with most of our work, you'll build on the awareness created from previous exercises. Review the Ability Transition on p. 41 and p. 46 before starting this exercise.

1 Start in *Standing Meditation*.

2 Begin slowly bouncing on the balls of your feet. Your heels should come completely off the ground during the bounce. At no time should

Step 2

you lose your connection to the ground through the balls of your feet. Let your arms hang relaxed at your sides, elbows straight and not locked. Your wrists should be relaxed so that the motion of your body up and down shakes and flexes your wrists. The exercise creates a rhythmic motion in your body as you bounce. Feel your arms as pendulums; let them swing. Let your wrists flex. As you bounce, you will become immediately aware of your balance or lack of it.

3 It is important to continue bouncing for at least one minute, and then stop.

Ask yourself, "Where is my weight? Where is my breath?" If you are like most people, your weight probably shifted back in your body to where it is normally while standing (in the heels). In this position, you are misaligned and must therefore tighten various muscles to compensate for this misalignment. This tension is then transferred into your abdomen as it attempts to hold your center over your feet. For this reason, it may be difficult to maintain deep abdominal breathing while doing the exercise.

By this time you should be acutely aware of how a very small imbalance in your body is multiplied when you add motion to it. Were your calf muscles working hard? Did you feel how, when you lost your balance, your muscles immediately tightened to try and regain it? And after a very short time, did you feel that muscle begin to ache?

Take a moment and put yourself in your horse's shoes. Think of how much muscle he must use to compensate for your lack of balance. Remember the imbalance you have on the ground you have in the saddle—the only difference is you don't feel it, but your horse does. With this in mind, how many times have you thought that your horse was being naughty or "he just doesn't like to go to the right," when actually he was compensating for your imbalance that impedes his ability to move freely and respond to your aids? Don't feel bad, because the solution is at hand, or at your feet.

4 Now start to bounce again. This time start very slowly, by just lifting your heels off the ground.

5 Relax your calf muscles and let your heels drop back down.

6 Repeat this action several times until you can "let go" with your muscles and your heels drop with a thud to the ground.

Notice that your imbalance usually occurs when you're lifting up, not when you drop.

Are you using too many muscles to lift your body? If so, this will pull you out of alignment.

7 Try a few seconds of abdominal breathing before you lift your heels off the
ground. Inhale as you lift your heels off the ground and exhale as you drop.
Within a few tries, you should feel lighter on the lift and heavier on the drop.

8 Begin to bounce again. Compare your balance with the beginning of the exercise.
Is your balance significantly better than in the beginning?

After you've stopped the bouncing, focus your mind on your hands. Listen to them for one minute.

Do you feel the sensation of electricity or tingling in them? What you feel is your chi.

Focus all your intent toward this sensation. Can you feel it moving? Does it move up your arms? Can you feel it in the balls of your feet?

This is a great warm-up and can be done before and after you ride. Try this one in the morning when you first wake up, to help shake off the sleep and start your day balanced.

> *Rider Insight, Lolly: Lolly had experienced carpal tunnel syndrome for fifteen
> years. When she practiced Wrist Shaking, she felt fire shooting down her wrists
> and out her fingertips. She was experiencing the stretching and relaxing of her
> tendons and muscles as they moved through the restricted area in her wrist. Doing
> this exercise, along with a few others in this book, helped her regain strength and
> range of motion in her hands and wrists. (She tells her full story in chapter 8, p. 227.)*

Ah-Ha!

With practice you will be able to bounce longer without getting tired. You will be able to maintain deep abdominal breathing throughout. The sense of well-being and calm attained by focusing on the chi will come sooner and last longer.

Tai Chi masters say that the chi is directed only by the mind and will go where the mind goes. Also, great healing properties have been accredited to the manipulation of chi. I would ask you to diligently practice listening to the chi every time you do this exercise.

Many marvelous and mysterious powers have been given to the development and mastery of one's own chi. There are stories of Tai Chi masters throwing their chi out beyond their own bodies to knock over opponents without physically touching them. I cannot attest to the validity of these claims, because I have never seen any of these feats in person. However, I do know that I can focus on the sensation created by this exercise for a long period of time. When I finish this exercise, I feel a deep sensation of calm and clarity.

Ability Transition

The knowledge gained about your balance, weight distribution, and breath will begin to become apparent throughout the day and when you ride. You will be able to make adjustments in your body to maintain your balance before the tension sets in your muscles.

Reminder

When done regularly, this simple exercise will reveal a lifetime of knowledge about your body and balance.

Sink and Circulate the Chi

Riding Goals: Balance, Relaxation

When your breath is relaxed, even, and fluid, your horse can feel it, and he also will relax.

Function

This exercise teaches you to harmonize your breath and motion into one conscious flow. It teaches you how to continue breathing throughout a ride, regardless of the horse's behavior. Most riders tend to hold their breath just prior to giving an aid, if only for a moment. This holding causes the body to tense. Your horse can feel this tension and must compensate for it.

Intent

In this exercise, as with all the movements in this book, your mind directs the breath and the body. You also use your mind to create or remind yourself of certain positive feelings that help change your physical body. For instance, while opening your arms in the initial motions of this form, I suggest imagining that you are welcoming an old friend or loved one to your home. The energy is light and open, just as the movement should be.

Step-by-Step

1 Begin in *Standing Meditation.*

2 Slowly raise your arms up and out to your sides, keeping your palms faced forward and your thumbs pointed up. Continue to lift your arms in an arcing motion until your hands are at ear level.

3 While keeping your elbows in the same spot, relax and bend your elbows so that your hands circle up, around, and down past your face. Now your palms are facing down, with your hands at about chin level and 12 inches in front of you. Note that your elbows remain slightly bent.

Step 1: Two views

James On Your Shoulder

Find the rotation of your arm within the larger movement of the circles. When your breath matches the motion and you feel a tingling sensation in your hands during the exercise, you are circulating chi.

Visualize the chi moving from your center (your lower Dain Tian), back and upward through your spine up to your head. Your chi then moves back down the front of your body and returns to your center.

4 Continue to lower your hands as if you were pushing down on a ball filled with helium. This movement, in fact the entire exercise, should be soft and fluid; *even while in motion, create a feeling of stillness.*

5 As your hands reach your waist, roll each humerus (upper arm), which will cause your elbows to drop back to your sides. At the same time rotate your wrists, so that your palms now face up and are in front of your Dain Tian.

6 Pause in this position and take two or three slow abdominal breaths. With each breath expand the sphere of energy originating in your Dain Tian until you have filled a large ball of energy that now rests in your hands.

7 Slowly raise your arms up in front of your body, keeping your wrists and elbows slightly bent. Your arms should rise as if someone were lifting them by a string that is attached at your wrists. Continue lifting your arms until they are at the level of your heart and the middle Dain Tian.

Step 2

Step 3

Step 4

Steps 5 and 6

Step 7

8 Draw your hands toward your body by slowly bending and dropping your elbows simultaneously, until your hands are approximately one fist length in front of your chest. The palms of your hands should face downward at approximately 45 degrees.

9 Slowly and gently push your palms outward until your elbows are nearly straight.

10 Slowly allow your arms to drop down to the sides of your body, back into the beginning position.

Mounted

Repeat the above motions while on the longe line, in the round pen, or while at the walk in an arena. Notice how your horse relaxes. Pay attention to his breathing as you allow the slow, circular, rhythmic motion to relax your breath and body (see photos).

You are opening *Gate 4: The Back of the Heart.* You already do things in your life that open this gate. When you hug someone you love, you spread your shoulder blades as you wrap your arms around them. You're also softening *Gate 3: The Front of the Heart.*

You make your arms rounder and couple their motion with your breath. Feel like you expand in your back: imagine that you have a tiny purple dot between your shoulders—now you make it bigger by expanding between your shoulders.

When you open your gates, your horse will feel it. He will be more likely to collect and round his back under you. When your gates are closed, your horse won't come up into you.

Ah-Ha!

When you lift your arms correctly, they will feel light—even weightless. This feeling happens when you maintain proper structural alignment throughout the motion and use only the muscles necessary to lift your arms.

Ability Transition

You will notice that your breathing becomes deeper and slower as you practice. As your mind, breath, and body begin to move in harmony, you may experience a sense of calm and well-being. The circling of your arms will feel bigger and rounder with practice.

Performing the steps for
Sink and Circulate
the Chi while mounted.

Reminder

Do not force your breath down. You want the breath to sink deep into the abdomen naturally; forcing it down will create tension in your body. Force creates tension, and this is the habit you're trying to break by retraining yourself. So, breathe with ease and relaxation. When you breathe in, imagine you are smelling a flower.

Horse Stance and Wall Sitting

This exercise trains you to ride with the muscles of the backs of your legs and gluteus muscles relaxed. When these muscles are tightened, their attachment point at your pelvis is tight and hard, which restricts the fluid motion of your pelvis and separates you from your saddle and horse.

Function

This exercise teaches you to breathe continuously, gently, and deeply into your abdomen while strengthening the muscles in your legs and abdomen. While it is absolutely necessary for you to use certain muscles in your legs and abdomen while riding, you don't need to employ all the muscles in those areas. In fact, the overuse of certain dominant muscles in these areas leads to restricted motion in your hips and lower back, which in turn separates you from your horse. This exercise helps you identify which muscles are unnecessarily, unconsciously engaged while in a riding position. It also teaches you how to "let go of" and relax those muscles, while using only the muscles necessary for balance.

In addition, you'll also learn to move your lower lumbar region independently of the rest of your body. This will change your balance, and this new motion, originating in your center, will help you sit the trot and canter.

Intent

The exercise trains your mind to stay focused and calm when your body begins to tire. Through focus and awareness, you use your mind to direct your breath down into your abdomen and lower back (your Ming Meng).

Step-by-Step

There are two parts to this exercise:

Part One: *Horse Stance* builds an understanding of what happens in your body unconsciously while in a riding position, which typically leads to a separation of horse and rider.

Part Two: *Wall Sitting* trains your body to move more effectively while in the *Horse Stance* position.

Horse Stance

1 You'll start from a standing position. I would like you to put yourself into—as closely as you can—the position you are in while riding.

Take your time. Close your eyes and see yourself on your horse, and really make sure you are in your riding position. Ask yourself, "Are my legs bent enough? Is my back straight? Where are my elbows; my hands?" Take a few moments to feel your body in this position and become aware of any tension in your body. Is there tightness in your lower back? Are your legs straining to support your weight in this position? Is your abdomen relaxed? Is your breathing shallow and up in your chest?

2 Now try and let go of the tension. Relax and don't change the position, but just try to relax into it. Chances are if you begin to relax for a moment, it will not last. Very soon your body will likely become tense. This happens because you're inherently in a structurally weak position. I'll explain the reasons why.

Look down at the space between your knees and ask yourself, "Is my horse really that skinny?" Approximately 99 percent of the thousands of riders I've worked with stand with their knees far too close together when I ask them to assume their riding position. You may think that all you have to do is move your knees out a bit, or you say, "My knees go where the width of my horse puts them." You would be correct as long as you were on the ground, but things change when you mount your horse. On your horse, you ask him not only to support your weight, but also make up for your imbalances. I believe that your stance is crucial, and it plays a major role in keeping you from a soft and connected seat.

3 Try this little experiment: assume your riding position with your knees closer together, and with two fingers reach back under your seat and place your fingers on your seat bones. Can you feel the muscles and tendons that lie over the top of the bones? No? That's because in this position the muscles and tendons are relaxed and not in use. This relaxation would be great if this were truly the position you were in while riding.

Begin in your riding position with your legs bent and your back straight. Check if your knees are too close together by placing two fingers on your seat bones, as described in Step 3.

Step 5

Now, while keeping your fingers on your seat bones, push your knees out into the position that the width of your horse puts them in. Notice how the muscles and tendons tighten and push your fingers away from the bone. This tightening is what happens when you sit in the saddle and your horse moves your knees apart. It pushes you out of the saddle with tension between you and the horse. Most riders unconsciously compensate for this by arching their lower back, putting their body out of alignment. Arching your back completely compromises your structural support and balance.

5 Take another moment and play with this position. See how by moving your knees and arching your back, you not only change the state of the muscles and tendons in your seat but you also affect your balance.

6 In this *Horse Stance*, have a friend softly push on your chest. Are you easily pushed out of balance?

Feel how your body tenses against the push. Having a friend push against you simulates the effects of an outside force applied to your position. The pushing produces the same reaction in your body that the movement of the horse underneath you creates when you sit in a weak position. Notice that as the push is continued, your body attempts to maintain balance in the same way it does when riding out of balance. You immediately hold your breath and tense up, your elbows begin to rise, and either your chest pushes forward or your hips move forward toward your friend. When this happens your lower back will tighten and your hands squeeze. The last thing you will do in an attempt to keep from falling is to reach out and grab your friend's arms—just as you tend to "grab" or hold the reins when things go poorly in the saddle.

Caution

This initial position is extremely important to this exercise being effective and safe. An incorrect starting position will result in undue stress upon your knees and back.

Now let's work on developing a better Horse Stance. For this exercise, you will need a sturdy, flat wall to sit back against, with a floor that is level and not slippery.

1 Stand with your back to the wall. Place your heels approximately 12 to 15 inches away from the wall. To find the optimum position: (a) place your right heel against the wall; (b) reach down and place your right fist on the floor in front of the toes of your right foot—the side of your fist away from the wall now marks where you should place your right heel; (c) stand back up and move your right heel to this location, moving your left foot the same distance from the wall; (d) place your feet one shoulder-width apart and parallel to each other.

Step 2

2 Slowly sit back against the wall and lower your body so that your thighs are parallel to the ground. Your upper and lower legs should form a 90-degree angle. Your hands rest on your knees, which are directly over your feet. Your back is flat against the wall.

3 Rest the back of your head against the wall. Take a moment in this position to feel your body. What muscles are you using? Is your breath relaxed and deep?

4 Slowly roll your tailbone off the wall so that your lower back (your Ming Meng) pushes back into the wall. At the same time, roll your shoulders forward away from the wall so that more of your lower back presses into the wall.

Step 4

5 Hold this position for two full deep breaths. As you inhale, direct your breath with your mind down into your lower back. Think of your abdomen as a balloon, expanding out in all directions.

6 Slowly lean back with your shoulders as you allow your tailbone to move back against the wall. Feel the arch in your lower spine return to its resting position as it pulls your lower back away from the wall.

7 Repeat Steps 4 through 6 until the motion is clean and fluid (review the Eight Principles, p. 16). As your body becomes stronger and more relaxed with the movement, increase the length of time you're in the "pulled-away-from-the-wall" position.

Step 6

Ah-Ha!

For many of you, the first thing you will feel is a burning in your thighs. This is a good thing. It means that the right muscles are at work. Your thighs are the root of your waist, and they need to be strong and tension-free. Any unnecessary tension in the thighs leads to restricted motion in the pelvis.

As you pull your shoulders and tailbone away from the wall, you will feel the muscle on the inside of your upper leg down near your knee start to work. Again, this is good. This muscle, the vastus medialus, helps stabilizes your knee and upper leg while riding. If you use your whole thigh to stabilize your leg, you only succeed in squeezing the horse and restricting the movement of your pelvis.

Ability Transition

When you practice, you will find that it becomes easier to keep your abdominal breathing slow and deep. It is my experience that when I control my breath, I control my body and mind. When I first began training in this exercise, I noticed a sort of mental panic when I felt the burn in my legs in this stance. It was not my muscles that were giving out, but my mind. The minute I began to focus on the burn, I lost focus on my breath, which disconnected me from the rest of my body.

Be sure that you aren't dropping, tucking, or tilting your tailbone. You are moving your spine and pelvis. See the related exercise in chapter 4, *Open the Ming Meng* (p. 99).

As with most of the exercises in this book, there are many levels of teachings. Remember that the great treasures lie just under the surface of these seemingly simple forms. While riding you will start to notice that your center moves more, yet you will feel more balanced and centered.

Reminder

If you feel any pain in your knees or back, stop immediately and check your position and alignment. In the beginning, don't try to do too many repetitions or hold the position for an extended period of time.

Mounted

Practice this exercise before a ride to warm up the muscles of your spine and legs.

When you ride at the posting trot, apply the feeling of the *Horse Stance*. Think about your legs and their position in the sitting and rising phases of your posting. Actively remember the feeling of support you felt in your legs, seat, and back during *Wall Sitting*: an awareness of muscular presence in your legs; an awareness of softness in your seat; and an awareness of a back free of all tension. Your goal is to carry the awareness you gained on the wall over to sitting in the saddle. Don't surrender your structural alignment for a soft seat. Be soft, but achieve this through balanced alignment rather than muscular effort.

Walking Backward

Riding Goals: Awareness, Balance, Body Control, Influencing the Horse

This exercise has two main goals:

First, you will develop coordination in your body by walking backward— the opposite of what you are accustomed to. All the muscles that usually play the dominant role in walking and riding will need to follow the lead of your less-used muscles. This motion develops balance and sensitivity of both the individual muscles and your body as a whole.

Second, you will learn to trust all your senses, not just your eyes. Most of us only believe what we can see. This is apparent in the majority of riders that I have observed who spend a considerable amount of time looking down at the horse to see if they have changed leads, collected, or are posting on the correct diagonal. These riders often continue to look at the horse, even after their instructor has pointed out and proven to them how unstable and weak the body is with the head down. This is simply a bad habit that we need to overcome by retraining.

Function

This exercise's most important function is to increase your awareness of the power of your intent. It also builds a certain level of trust between mind and body. By moving in the direction opposite of where you are looking, and not allowing yourself to look back, you force your body to trust what your mind knows. On completing this exercise you will experience a change in your reality and perception of your environment and how your intent has the power to move everything you see.

Intent

Use your mind to manipulate your intent and perception. When you first stop walking backward, everything you see will appear to be moving toward you. This may challenge your balance at first, but you will use your mind to imagine you are floating an inch off the ground, and instead of being pushed over, you will feel as if you are floating and bringing your environment to you. This technique can be used to perfect the timing of your transitions. It's one of the most powerful exercises I've ever experienced.

Step-by-Step

The actual exercise is very simple—you walk backward for at least five minutes.

1. Stand in an empty riding arena or any quiet place where you can see the entire path on which you will be walking.

It helps if the place is familiar to you. It is very important before you begin walking that you can look and see there is nothing to trip over or fall down into.

2. Start walking backward. There are two things you must do while walking backward: (a) Keep your head straight forward, resisting the temptation to look back over your shoulder to see where you are going. You have already seen for yourself that there is nothing to trip you up. Trust yourself, and develop your other senses.

(b) When you step backward, try to keep your feet parallel and shoulder-width apart at all times. This will help to develop the weaker muscles in the legs and enhance your balance.

3. After walking for at least five minutes stop and focus on what you see. Is everything in sight moving toward you, knocking you off balance? Do you feel as though you are losing your balance backward?

4. Now change your focus and align your body into *Standing Meditation*.

5. Expand your crown upward. Imagine that you are floating an inch off the ground in perfect structural alignment.

Does it now seem as if you are flying or floating toward any point you choose in your field of vision?

6. Stand for one minute or longer and experience this new reality.

Later in the book, you will recreate this experience while riding. The experience will aid in the timing of transitions from one gait to another.

Ah-Ha!

With a little practice, you will be able to call up this incredible focus at will. You will find that when you stop walking and stand in place, you will immediately begin to float.

Ability Transition

As you walk more and more, your stride will become smoother and longer and you'll develop a rhythmic gait to your movement.

Reminder

Don't look back. Fight the urge to look, because this ability to focus will later help you to not look down while riding. Keep your feet parallel while walking.

> *Rider Insight, Trish: "The best part of the weekend was the Walking Backward exercise. It was so powerful for me because I have a tendency to rush into things. Recognizing the world was moving toward me instead of me rushing to get to something was incredible. Now when I feel myself get impatient, I remember that it's out there waiting to happen and I can refocus and be intentional about whatever it is I'm waiting for. It has sparked some interesting conversations with my friends, who have pointed out that maybe I don't have to wait—whatever I am looking for is right there ready to happen, and I just have to reach out for it. However I look at it, the exercise has helped me to relax and start to move in the professional and personal directions I want, rather than spinning my wheels and going nowhere fast."*

Walking backward makes some people feel giddy. One person told me she was transported back to mind-bending feelings she experienced in the 1960s, and she asked, "Is this legal?"

Summary

You've begun to experience the effortless mind-body connection in this first series of exercises. You're *born* with this mind-body connection. Watch an infant respond to someone tickling her toe. Her whole body moves.

Two Types of Mind

There are two types of mind: the sensing or spiritual mind (yi) and the intellectual, analytical mind (shen). The exercises in this chapter help you experience your yi mind, feeling your body rather than intellectualizing about what you're doing. The more you think about your motion, the greater chance you'll get "stuck" thinking it out rather than allowing yourself to experience sensations.

> "Don't try to understand yourself with physical seeing."
>
> (adapted from Deng Ming-Dao, from *365 Tao Daily Meditations*)

Use your mind's eye to see within your body as well as outside the body. Remember how you felt before you experienced *Walking Backward*, and then what you felt after. This exercise helps you open up your third eye, because your intent is behind you. This same experience—this faith—will apply to the exercises to come. You'll be able to visualize the effects of the exercises. It's not just faith alone, but also the other tools you'll apply. Every aspect of each exercise has a physical reality, and a physical change takes place that you can measure.

Remember this image, and realize that you, too, always possess that connection. With time and practice, the satisfying moments of deep mind-body connection will come more quickly and last longer.

You'll find it's a challenge to maintain the mind-body connection, because it's easy to be pulled out of this state by distracting thoughts, physical bad habits, or being startled. As you practice, you may even experience moments that frighten you. Don't worry about these reactions; they're entirely normal. Just relax and keep working.

These exercises also started to make you aware of your breath and your intent. Now you have begun to use your breath as the vehicle that takes your mind into your body. By becoming mindful of your breath, you'll prolong and maintain that connection.

In the exercises to come, you'll build on your new awareness of mind and body. You will develop mindfulness of your breath. Your breath and your intent are your most versatile and powerful tools in riding.

The awareness gained from *Walking Backward* prepares you for the subtleties of future exercises, which include using your breath to maintain your own awareness and posture as well as to influence your horse. You will then learn to use your intent to visualize a change in your body prior to it happening—for instance when changing gaits. It's necessary for you to visualize it before it happens. By visualizing, I don't mean developing your logical understanding. This work with mind and body is actually a form of meditation.

What's Next

In chapter 4: "Expanding Our Perspective: Tai Chi's Healing Path and the Gift of the Horse," we will continue to build the foundation of the rest of the book. We will do this foundation work both physically—for instance, doing the first of a series of therapeutic *Laing Gong* exercises—and intellectually, as we consider a variety of perspectives on riding, including balance, injury, and control. We will look at strategies to working with forces larger than ourselves (such as our horses), and finally we'll briefly discuss Tai Chi and other Asian arts.

Expanding Our Perspective

4

Tai Chi's Healing Path and the Gift of the Horse

IN THIS CHAPTER I AM GOING TO CONSIDER A NUMBER of influences on horsemanship to which you might not ordinarily give much thought—but all of which can have a profound effect on your well-being and your riding. These influences range from the psychological to the physical.

Horse as Mirror, Horse as Healer

Horses are a perfect mirror of what is going on inside the rider physically and emotionally. When you are sitting on your horse, his movement is a natural reflection of your own state of physical balance. The horse's attitude and disposition is an accurate reflection of a rider's emotional and spiritual state.

Native American tradition teaches that Great Spirit first placed the animals upon the earth as our teachers. They are closer to nature than the "two-leggeds." The medicine of Horse is that of the healer, and its symbolism is progress of psyche and inner spirit. The horse is incapable of lying. This makes him a very honest partner who offers us an opportunity for learning to be more truthful with others and ourselves.

Let's explore more of the background teachings of *Ride from Within*.

Laing Gong Exercises

Laing Gong is a complete set of therapeutic exercises designed to unblock and create a strong flow of internal energy (chi) throughout the body. This flow is essential to our health and longevity; *Laing Gong* means, in fact, "ultimate health exercise." Beyond the general health benefits of these exercises are gains of particular interest to riders: Laing Gong enhances range of motion in your joints while maintaining the structural balance essential in riding, and through Laing Gong, you develop highly sensitive control of your physical body as well as focus and concentration of the mind.

These exercises are the best way I know of quickly and effectively increasing your body's ability to ride. Remember there is a vital difference between knowing, understanding, and visualizing, and being able to do something physically; your goal is to learn to ride better, not just think about riding better. These exercises will be part of your ongoing work to take what you learn mentally and bring that learning into action in your body.

The Ideas Behind Laing Gong

Your chi meridians and channels function like hoses through which chi flows, much like water in a garden hose. The stretching done in Laing Gong blocks the flow of chi in the meridians—like squeezing a garden hose in the middle—creating back pressure. Upon releasing the stretch, the trapped chi surges forward with much more force than it would naturally have on its own. This surge of chi flushes the meridian, dislodging any blockages. Because of the back pressure created, it is important not to hold the stretch of any Laing Gong exercises for more than one second so as not to damage the meridians. I call this the one-second stretch rule, and I'll remind you of this from time to time. (See chart of meridians in the *Appendix,* p. 250)

You can feel chi in your body in a number ways—as heat, as a pins-and-needles sensation, or even the sensation of electricity moving through the arm. Do not be frightened by these sensations—they are natural and healing. In the beginning, the sensations may be strong. With repeated practice, the intensity of these sensations generally subsides, as the channels have been opened and the chi now flows more freely.

Laing Gong exercises are simple movements designed to unblock your chi. They will help you feel the energy that powers your entire body. Laing Gong is divided into six series. Each series contains six exercises. Each series focuses on healing and strengthening specific areas of the body.

• Series 1–Neck and Shoulders
• Series 2–Back
• Series 3–Hips, Knees, and Ankles
• Series 4–Joints
• Series 5–Tendons and Connective Tissue
• Series 6–Healing Internal Disorders

You'll practice Laing Gong exercises on the ground and from the saddle in the coming chapters. On the next page is an exercise I suggest you practice now.

Laing Gong Palm and Fist

The largest concentration of acupressure and acupuncture points on any given meridian is located from the finger tips to just behind the wrist. The hands reveal tension in the body by the way the fingers move and are held in relaxation. The following exercise will help you understand the precise yet simple movement of the Laing Gong forms and how there is more to each exercise than first meets the eye.

Step-by-Step

1 Hold your hand open with the fingers together and pointing away from your body. The thumb should be at a 90-degree angle from the fingers. The back of the hand and the forearm create a straight line.

2 Holding the hand in this position, feel what is going on. Do you feel tension in the fingers, thumb, wrist, or forearm? Breathe. Relax. Take a moment and let go of the unnecessary tension. The fingers and the thumb should feel as if they are stretching away from the palm of the hand. With the hand held in this manner, the center of the palm (see photo) should be slightly concave and soft.

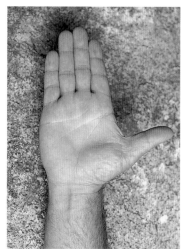

Steps 1 and 2

3 Slowly close the opened hand into a fist by rolling your fingers down into the palm of the hand and at the same time close the thumb over the outside of your fingers to form the Laing Gong fist. The fist is not clenched; do not squeeze it tight.

4 Once again search for unwanted tension. Is your fist tight? Are the muscles in your forearm tense? If there is tension, let go of it. As you release the tension, does the flatness of the back of the hand and forearm change?

5 Repeat this slow closing and opening of the palm to a fist several times. Find a rhythm in the stretching out of the thumb and fingers from the palm. With just a little practice you will begin to feel energy pumping into your hand. Remember to follow the one-second stretch rule.

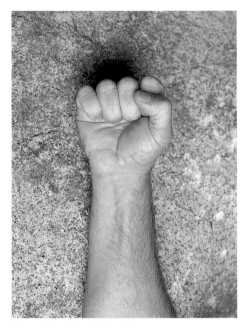 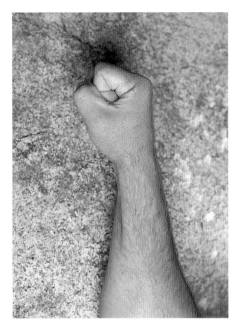

Steps 3 and 4: Two views

The main goal of this exercise is for you to begin to see how much unnecessary tension you create when you move—even when performing the simplest of tasks. Once you become aware of this tension, practicing the exercise then teaches you to let go of it and move with greater ease.

Laing Gong exercises also help develop your ability for independent motion, such as moving your spine without moving your limbs. You'll be better able to follow the motion of your horse in your trunk without setting your arms and legs into motion. Every motion is generated from your center, so you can create motion in the horse from inside your body while the outside remains quiet.

The Horse's Natural Balance

Horses move in natural balance, as you see when watching your horse at liberty. Natural balance is distinct from purely athletic balance. Natural balance precedes athletic balance; it is innate in all horses and derives from their integral connection to the natural world, to the earth.

All horses, just like any other sort of athlete, vary in their talent. Some horses move in better athletic balance than others—both at liberty and under saddle. Every horse has to learn how to move in athletic balance when carrying a rider—this is one of the most important skills that a trainer can help a horse develop. Because this book focuses on riders, let's assume that you're riding a trained horse that can move in athletic balance while carrying a rider.

When we change our focus to the rider, I find that the majority of riders tend to unbalance their horses. I have never seen a horse that has less balance than his rider. Your horse compensates for your imbalance—he supports your imbalance and in doing so becomes imbalanced himself.

> *Rider Insight, Judy: While attending one of my clinics, Judy became aware during the groundwork just how restricted the movement of her body had become. She had injured her back four years earlier, and she said that she had only been relatively pain-free for the last year. However, her horse's back was now so tender and sore that he could barely tolerate her sitting in the saddle. Judy could not trace the horse's problems to any disease, injury, or accident. She had owned the horse since birth and was a good, loving owner. She had sought chiropractic help,*

Tai Chi's Internal and External Forces

Americans tend to think of Tai Chi as a slow-motion "health" exercise. What they often don't realize is that Tai Chi is a martial art. In Tai Chi for the equestrian, the secrets of its power are hidden in its motions. The motions of a Tai Chi form are actually martial arts techniques strung together based on a series of attack and counter maneuvers. While I will not focus on the martial aspect of each motion, I will explore the underlying forces that are at the heart of how Tai Chi works.

changed the horse's feed, and used massage. She was considering retiring him if it meant keeping him out of pain.

I cautiously suggested that her horse might have developed his back problems by compensating for hers. After watching the two ride for a few minutes, it was clear that the lack of movement and rigidity in Judy's body was causing the horse to brace against Judy's force. This caused him to hold with muscles that should be relaxed in movement, and therefore created misalignment in his spine. Many horses would not have tolerated this unfair balancing act and simply would have resisted being ridden at all.

By our working on Judy's body movement and breathing, she was able to improve her balance and relax her horse. By no means can Tai Chi "fix" a problem years in the making in a one-hour session—it takes a lot of consistent work to cure such an issue of balance. The good news is that Judy is no longer treating her horse's symptoms and has discovered the root cause of his pain.

Let's say, over time, you've slowly lost your natural balance. Bad habits moved in and have disturbed your original, natural alignment. You may have forgotten what it feels like to be well-aligned and balanced—both naturally and athletically. The good news is that you can still regain these abilities and feelings.

Use the exercises in this book both on the ground and on your horse; they will help you develop your natural balance and your athletic balance. Remember that your goals are physical and spiritual. Don't underestimate the power of the horse as healer.

When you understand how Tai Chi works as a martial art, you can begin to see its direct relationship with riding. Understanding the difference between internal and external force is essential. In classic Tai Chi thought, internal energy is synonymous with chi, and its application in force is called *fah jing*. *Fah* means "to project" and *jing* means "internal power."

Internal Force

Internal force refers to the way you generate power through your entire body. Your internal forces produce your position and keep your body in rhythm. You create internal force and direct it from the center (your Dain Tian) of your body.

> "The internal energy should be extended, and vibrate like the beat of a drum. The spirit should be condensed in toward the center of your body."
>
> *(Tai Chi Classics)*

For your purposes, consider internal force as any motion originating from your center directed by your mind. The motion works in harmony with the natural laws described in chapter 2. You direct your internal forces, starting with your mind directing your breath. You breathe through your abdomen, and you gain control of your center (see *Dain Tians,* p. 19).

As you sit on the horse, you redirect or influence the internal force of the horse with your internal force. This is the meaning of joining energy. Ideally when you sit relaxed, aligned, and balanced, your horse will move by using only his natural, internal energy, rather than having to use external force or strength.

External Force

External force is any power you create using muscle to move an isolated part of your body, such as when you squeeze your thighs to hold yourself onto the saddle or pull back on the reins with your arms by tensing your shoulders and tightening the biceps.

External force disconnects one part of your body from the rest through tension. When the motion of any part of your body does not move in concert with the overall flow of momentum in the body as a whole, it becomes disconnected and your power is fragmented. For example, picture yourself riding and maintaining your center over the horse's center (joined). You are moving your whole body in rhythmic waves of force. However, when you apply a leg aid, you tighten—and tense—your thigh to produce the aid. In creating that force, you have disconnected your thigh from the flow of momentum and natural power of the body.

Remember when you use external force, whether it's to maintain your own balance or influence your horse, you disconnect from the greater flow of your combined energy. Not only do you disrupt the natural rhythm of your body, but you also interfere with the horse's natural rhythm.

You are the horse's "guest." You sit on his weakest point—the center of his spine—suspended between his structural supports, his legs—by only the strength of his muscles. You sit in the saddle and govern his movements through your influence.

Rider-Based Issues

Injuries and Compensation

Most people have at some time in their life been injured, and if so, their bodies carry the memories of these past traumas. Some people are conscious of these memories; others are not. Whether conscious or not, everyone who has been injured compensates for the injury to one degree or another.

If you have been hurt, you may find that in compensating you create imbalance, misalignment, and stress in your body. You compensate both mentally and physically, and both types directly affect your horse. Here are some real examples from friends and students of mine.

One friend, who had been riding only a few years, was on the trail when her horse spooked and bolted. She held on as best she could for nearly a quarter mile, until she was thrown as her horse turned to miss a fence. She was very lucky that she escaped with only a few bruised ribs when her body came to a stop against the fence. Her horse ran off and was not found for three days. He was also fine—a bit scratched up and dirty, but none the worse for wear.

I first began to work with the two of them in an indoor arena, and they looked relaxed and moved quite well together. Then we moved to the outdoor arena, which had no fence, just a rail on the ground defining the edges.

The rider became tense and tight in her upper body, and she began to hunch over her horse. The entire change in her physical body was because she was afraid to lose control, and this is certainly understandable. The problem was that the position of her body created not the connection and confidence she wanted, but exactly the opposite: disconnection and fear. I could tell by watching her horse that he was reacting to her position and fear by becoming distracted, and increasingly paying more attention to what was "out there" than to her. She was a good example of how emotional compensation affects the body.

Asian Healing Arts

Traditional Chinese medicine is based on the concept that chi is the animating force of life, and without it there is no life. Practitioners believe that everything contains chi—plants, animals, rocks, and air—and that there is a free flow of chi through all things in the universe. Sickness is the result of either a lack of chi or its stagnation. The goal of acupuncture and acupressure is to stimulate and move this chi through the body. Acupuncture uses needles applied to specific points on the chi meridians in the body to move your unseen life force. Acupressure uses finger pressure or massage to stimulate chi flow.

You and Your Horse: Food for Thought

Finish these sentences to help you assess your strengths and weaknesses:

I can ride _____ minutes a day.

I have _____ (more/less) energy after I ride than before I started.

My horse feels _____ (tense/relaxed) when I start to ride.

When my horse shies, I react by _____.

When I see myself ride in photographs or videos, I am smiling ___ percent of the time.

Now answer yes or no:

When my horse evades my aids, I become more active with my hands, legs, and seat.

When I half-halt my horse, I tense up.

I am aware of my body's breathing when I ride.

I am aware of my body's rhythm when I ride.

I am aware of my horse's breathing when I ride.

An example of physical compensation is that of a cowboy I worked with, who had been living with mild but constant back pain for years. He was in his fifties and rode mostly for pleasure by this time in his life. During a weekend lesson, I noticed he always rode with one hand on the reins and one hand firmly placed on his thigh. When I asked him why, he said it was just comfortable and a habit. Upon further investigation I learned of his back pain, and we came to discover that his hand on his thigh was really a way to brace his back against the motion of the horse.

The problem as I saw it was that his bracing was actually prolonging the back injury by protecting it. By keeping one hand on his thigh, he was actually bypassing his spine. The force created by the movement of his horse was transferred through his arm and hand into his leg and then into his seat. Pretty smart on his part! In bypassing the spine, his lower back did not have to negotiate the force down through it, and it remained tight and rigid. This compensation strategy kept the area "safe," but it also kept it from healing. Only through relaxing the smaller muscles of the lumbar can they move, heal, gain strength, and begin at another level to trust the brain again.

Innate Fear of Falling

We all have an innate fear of falling. Unless we have trained ourselves to overcome this fear, we carry it with us on and off the horse. I'm not suggesting that everyone who rides should first learn how to fall, although for some it would definitely help. However, I do believe that it is beneficial to understand how your body reacts to and compensates for this fear.

If you begin to lose your balance, your body immediately starts to tense up and you hold your breath. This tension is the body's attempt to hold itself in balance. Unfortunately, if you were not in alignment when you began to lose your balance, you have already compromised your structural support and you cannot rebalance yourself. Your next reaction is to reach out to hold onto something or someone, in an attempt to keep from falling further. If that is of no avail, you continue to fall and the last thing your body does before hitting the ground is to close its eyes—and then, thud.

In the saddle, if you begin to lose your balance even slightly, your body reacts with tension. This tightening of the abdomen (to protect the internal organs) causes you to hold your breath. If that does the trick and you catch your balance, no big deal. You just have to remember to breathe and let go of the tension in your abdomen and torso, and within a few strides you may regain your connection with your horse. If you cannot catch your balance, you next try to reach out to regain it. Typically your elbows jut out, your hands come up and out, and you push your head forward.

Practitioners of martial arts such as Tai Chi recognized early on the inevitability of falling and hitting the ground, and they realized that the only thing they truly had any control over was how they hit the ground. There is a saying in martial arts: "I'm not interested in hitting or kicking an opponent—I'm interested in capturing his spine. It is then just a matter of steps before he hits the ground. And the ground never misses and hits much harder than I."

In your own riding watch for the patterns of tensing and movement associated with the fear of falling. Realize that balance is the key to preventing falling in the first place, and Tai Chi can help you gain the alignment that underlies improved balance.

Control Issues

> *Rider Insight, Jenny:* "*Lack of power: that is our dilemma. If I just could get my horse to listen, to go where I tell her, to behave while I'm grooming her, to pay attention to my aids, and to stop scratching and pulling on the bit. Then I could focus on me, my breath, my body.*"

Some riders are under the illusion that their horses are in their lives for them to control. They feel that if they gain control over their horses, it will empower them in other areas of their lives where they feel out of control.

Horses *are* in our lives to empower and heal us, but not through our controlling them. No person is bigger and stronger than a horse, and without the advantage of tack most people could never ride. Horses are a gift, and our teachers, if we choose to listen.

Remember that the horse's gift to man is *healing*. Horses help you get inside yourself. They have the ability to expose your greatest weaknesses and strengths. You probably take better care of your horse than you do yourself. Your horse puts you in touch with your unconditional love and compassion. If you listen, he lets you know when you're carrying anger, frustration, and fear. By spending a few hours with your horse, you can let go of negative emotions. The next time you doubt the healing nature of the horse, spend a day at a therapeutic riding center and see the gift in action.

The whole of this book deals with the unintentional, unconscious disconnection of mind and body and how to regain this connection. This disconnectedness separates us not only from our true divine nature but also from our fellow man and woman. It keeps our eyes fixed on the symptoms as it distracts us from the root causes of our pain. If not for the gift of the horse, some of us would go through our lives never knowing we were separated from ourselves.

Your Horse as a Larger, Stronger Force

Your horse probably weighs between 900 and 1200 pounds. Stand beside him, and notice how much bigger and longer his head is than your head. Feel the size of his

Tai Chi and Other Asian Arts

You'll find similarities among Tai Chi, yoga, and transcendental meditation. I see hundreds of similarities, because all were developed to improve the human mind–body connection. Each discipline recognizes that this connection is vital when on the path of spiritual development. The goals of these arts are the same. The difference is that Tai Chi is bound by martial laws.

The history of riding as well as Tai Chi finds its roots in the martial arts. Cross country, dressage and jumping all developed from battle. You ride to the battle, you fight while mounted on your horse, and you ride back. Consider the great mounted battles of the past where there were as many as 80,000 warriors on each side. What chaos—what a challenge!

In the midst of this confusion, a warrior had to control his horse from his center because he held a sword in one hand and a shield in the other. He didn't rely on the reins to guide the horse. To survive, he had to control his horse's motion from his center. This concept might seem a bit much for those of you who enjoy a leisurely weekend trail ride. Nonetheless, the concepts in this book and their applications to riding have been proven over centuries of mounted warfare. Empires were built and conquered on the backs of horses by skilled warriors who understood the necessity of being one with their horse.

chest—the horse's lungs are huge. They fill most of his chest cavity, which can measure 72 inches, or 6 feet, around. If you saw a photograph of the two of you from the back, you'd see that his haunches are gigantic in comparison to yours! If you were dealing with a human of these proportions, I'm quite sure there would be much less telling and commanding and a lot more asking and listening.

When your horse moves, he must manage a tremendous amount of momentum due to his great weight. This momentum is a force that you can never stop with strength alone; at best you can only influence it. This limitation is demonstrated particularly clearly in jumping: once the horse has left the ground there is very little you can do until the horse lands.

Similarly, in the middle of a canter pirouette when the horse is at the apex of his upward motion, you can influence the way he comes to the ground, but you certainly can't stop the horse from coming down. The reason I point out the obvious in these examples is that as riders we sometimes believe that we always control the movements of our horse. In other words, we always lead, when in fact there are times that the best we can do is follow.

Power

Any horse can easily out-walk, out-jog, and outrun you. A horse can pull much more than his own massive weight. He can jump higher and farther than any human. The horse can also resist you in many ways, due to his superior size and strength. He can halt his forward impulsion, balk completely, back up, choose his own direction, rear, buck, or even lie down and refuse to get up.

In the saddle, you typically only feel his power when he pulls against your rein contact or bulges against your leg aid. On the ground, you are more likely to experience his awesome power, such as on those occasions where he might push you against a wall, or throw his weight back against the pressure of a lead rope.

Because horses are generous creatures, they allow you to mount them and direct them in activities like dressage, jumping, reining, and barrel racing. His size and strength, partnered with your skill and tact, make you and your horse partners in equestrian sport.

Your horse is an external force, separate from you but in many ways closer to the "supreme ultimate" that is Tai Chi. The horse moves with chi. He moves more in harmony with the universe, with fewer distractions than you. Your horse gives you a great rhythm to connect with—you feel the grace and power and are better for the experience. Consider your horse your teacher.

Summary

Now you have had your first taste of Laing Gong, the healing exercises that I will return to in chapter 6 in much greater depth. You have also explored some of the physical, psychological, and spiritual aspects of working with horses and riding. All this is food for thought for the curious equestrian. Let your curiosity draw you into all the work in this book. There is a great deal of fascinating work in the coming chapters.

What's Next

In chapter 5, "Your Breath: Learning to Breathe and Connect with Your Horse," you will deepen your understanding of Tai Chi by delving into one of its most fundamental tools: breath. Breath awareness and control is central to Tai Chi's goals of cultivating and balancing the flow of life force—chi—in your bodies. While this may sound mysterious or impractical, all the exercises in the next chapter have a direct application to riding—as well as, of course, enhancing your general health.

5 Your Breath

Learning to Breathe and Connect with Your Horse

THOUSANDS OF YEARS AGO IN CHINA, Taoist monks formulated the idea of an ultimate underlying power in the universe. They believed that this unseen power was responsible for life and order on earth and in the heavens. They called this power Chi, which means air, energy, motion, and power. Chi is the mother of Yin and Yang, and flows ceaselessly between two opposites; this flow joins the positive and negative at every level in the universe, and it is in this connection that we can find balance.

In Tai Chi we refer to chi as our internal energy. Tai Chi seeks to increase and balance the chi in our bodies through meditation and through move-ment. The exercises and breathing techniques in this chapter will engage

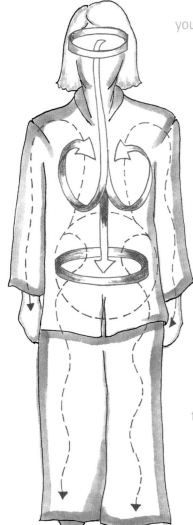

Breath and intent: the mind directs breath down into the abdomen where it is energized and stirs the chi (red arrows), and then directs the movement of the chi throughout the body (purple arrows).

your mind and body in both. When I use the word "meditation," I simply mean to focus on one thing with a calm and open mind. And, when I use the word "movement," I am speaking not just of the movement of your limbs, but also the movement of your breath.

Breathing is a perfect metaphor for life. Breathing *is* life. Breath is what we have in common with everything—the balance of nature and its pairing of Yin and Yang. For example, we share a perfectly complementary respiration with plants: they take in the carbon dioxide we exhale and produce oxygen; we take in the oxygen they give off and produce carbon dioxide.

And here's another example of Yin and Yang: there are only two breaths that don't come in pairs—your first and your last. At all other times, they are parts of a whole: inhalation and exhalation.

Breathing is for the most part an unconscious act. Thank goodness for that, because if we had to remember to breathe, most of us would not be here to read this book. You breathe in and out over 23,000 times a day. That's a lot of opportunity for practice and change.

Breathing is your body's natural metronome. Breathing sets the rhythm of your body, and rhythm is the key to timing. Without it you leave timing to chance, and timing is the key to transitions in speed, direction, and gait.

When you truly connect with your breath, your breathing synchronizes with your horse. Many times while I'm working with a rider on moving her breath down into the belly, as her breath drops, I hear the horse let out a sigh of relaxation. As you know, I often refer to the horse as your greatest teacher. If you listen to how your horse is breathing at any given gait, it will be a clue as to how you should breathe at that same gait.

If you're not in control of your breath, you're not in complete control of your body and balance. The question I most commonly ask riders is, "Where is your breath?" I ask this to remind them of the importance of breathing—especially when learning, because often when we are trying hard to do some new task, we tend to hold our breath. When you hold your breath you are cut off from your body. The exercises in this chapter help you discover where your breath is and how to better control your breathing.

Expanding Your Center through Breathing

You use your breath as a tool to expand your center. Physically, you can expand (increase the volume of) your center, your Dain Tian, by breathing. Abdominal breathing effectively expands your center, thereby making it easier to stay balanced. As your diaphragm pushes down on your internal organs, you learn to let go with the external muscles around your abdomen and pelvis. This letting go allows for freer movement of your joints in those areas, making it easier to stay with your horse.

You can't expand your center with force, and you can't develop muscles to expand your center. As far as your muscles are concerned, expanding your center means letting go of the tension held in your abdomen, and one of the most effective ways to release this tension is through abdominal breathing. Your center, you may be surprised to learn, can extend outside your body because your center incorporates not just bone and muscle but also breathe, awareness, and intent, all of which can expand into the space around you.

Chinese Tai Chi master Ma Yueh-liang, who was an expert in "Push Hands" (a two-man form of sparring in Tai Chi), said, "How can I be defeated when I can put my center behind you? How can you ever uproot me when my center is bigger than both of us, and it's behind you?" Ma Yueh-liang had 60 years of daily training. He was able to stand on one leg, and no one could uproot him. Imagine how balanced you'd be if you could put your center under your horse, or if you expanded your center so much that it encompassed you and your horse.

You can only expand your center through abdominal breathing and developing that combination of awareness and intent that I discussed in chapter 2. One of your goals is to transform your everyday breathing to match an old saying in Tai Chi: "Breathe in as if you're smelling a flower; breathe out as if you're playing a flute."

Imagine your center is a balloon that expands as you breathe air down into it.

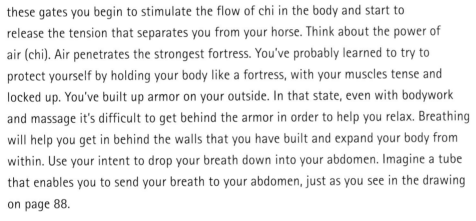

As an infant, you naturally breathed from your abdomen. Unfortunately, at around age five or six, you—like most children—probably began to breathe up in your chest. The good news is that you knew how to breathe into the belly once a long time ago, and now you just need to relearn, to remember how.

Abdominal breathing is also your first key to opening your gates. The first two you can open with breath are those of your center, Gate 1: The Dain Tian, and Gate 2: The Ming Meng. By opening these gates you begin to stimulate the flow of chi in the body and start to release the tension that separates you from your horse. Think about the power of air (chi). Air penetrates the strongest fortress. You've probably learned to try to protect yourself by holding your body like a fortress, with your muscles tense and locked up. You've built up armor on your outside. In that state, even with bodywork and massage it's difficult to get behind the armor in order to help you relax. Breathing will help you get in behind the walls that you have built and expand your body from within. Use your intent to drop your breath down into your abdomen. Imagine a tube that enables you to send your breath to your abdomen, just as you see in the drawing on page 88.

You'll practice *opening all your gates* in the breathing exercises. Envision the gates lined up, one behind the other. You open them sequentially: you open the first to get to the second, the second to get to the third, and so on. That is, you open Gate 1: The Dain Tian before you open Gate 2: The Ming Meng, and with the opening of the Ming Meng you can then open Gate 3: The Front of the Heart. It progresses in this way through all Eight Gates. When your last gate, Gate 8: The Crown, is open, you can return to the Dain Tian and open it even more, then expand the Ming Meng more, and so on. One gate's opening or expansion makes possible the opening or expansion of the next.

Once you have become proficient at opening the Eight Gates in sequence through breathing and intent, you will no longer have to open them in sequence. With experience, you will be able to open any gate at any time by just asking with your intent. *Opening the gates* is a series of awarenesses, of realizations—and of these there is no end.

As I mentioned earlier, although my Tai Chi teacher, Wen Mei Yu has been practicing for 40 years, she says we can always let go of more. "Even after all these years," she told me one day, "I need to relax my fingers more." You can always move to another more subtle, more powerful, level.

Influencing the Horse with Your Breath

On the path of mind, breath, and body, breathing is the way you introduce the mind to the body to develop a more conscious mind-body connection. Your breath also connects you with your horse. Your breath is the first thing your horse hears, a wordless whisper, one of the subtle ways you communicate with your horse. Breathing may tell the horse more than your physical body does. When you're approaching a transition, do you hold your breath? If you do, you immediately begin to tense your body, and in doing so, you tell the horse that something is worrisome—and because he's a sensitive flight animal, he may prepare to run. At the very least you are distracting him from the task of being your graceful and balanced partner.

Inhale and bring your breath down into your abdomen, which should expand out from the spine in all directions, just as when you inflate an ordinary balloon it expands symmetrically. Asymmetrical expansion indicates the presence of tension.

When the wind blows a leaf into your arena, do you typically react by holding your breath? If you're startled, you breathe high and short into your chest—and so does your horse! When anything goes wrong and you hold your breath, you tell your horse that something bad *is* going on. Your fear may never disappear completely, but by keeping your breath down and relaxed you can lower your center into the horse for greater security. You exhale when the surprise is over. It's the sigh of relief, a natural relaxant. The sigh is you letting go.

Tension can also have internal causes, including fear, anger, resentment, stress, and frustration. When you come to the barn, check in with yourself before you ride to see if you carried any of these negative emotions in with you. If you did, release them before you ride by doing a brief warm-up of *Standing Meditation* (p. 37) and *Abdominal Breathing*, a new exercise I'll describe on page 90.

Regardless of the tension's origin, are you aware of the moments when you hold your breath? Rarely is it enough for me to say to a rider, "You're holding your breath." Remembering to breathe deeply is far easier to think about than to do. For most riders there is a pattern to their breath-holding. My experience from working with hundreds of riders is that they hold their breath when going into a transition or when the horse does not respond favorably to an aid.

Let's look at this a little closer and ask yourself if this could be you. You approach the transition and inhale and hold your breath when you begin to give the aid for the next gait. It could be that you hold it because you've tensed your muscles in giving the aid and in doing so you've lost your balance a bit. (And remember that most riders hold their breath as soon as they begin to lose their balance.) Or, perhaps you inhale and hold your breath because you're never sure of what your horse's response will be to an aid, and so you brace for a possible overreaction. In either case, when you've completed the transition and realize that you weren't breathing, you exhale to relax.

Here's a test: take a deep breath, hold your breath, and listen to your body. Hold your breath as long as you possibly can, and feel the tension rise up in your body. Tension rises—relaxation sinks. Have you ever felt this same sensation while riding?

Because tension rises in your body, to relax you must let go of tension. Tension doesn't disappear. It seeks ground, just as electricity seeks the easiest path to earth. Imagine tension—like electricity—traveling down through your bones. Whether you are on your feet or mounted, abdominal breathing helps direct the released tension down through your body to the ground.

The automatic nature of breathing is both a strength and a weakness: because you don't have to think about it, you are not aware of its power. To change your breathing, you have to bring it out of the unconscious mind and into the conscious mind. If you're 50 years old, you've likely experienced over 45 years of shallow breathing. Changing your breathing will require daily practice.

Breath and Spirit

Breath is the root of spirituality. Nearly all religious sects use song as a means to praise or become closer to their creator. Have you ever sung in a choir? You focus on your breath, and you are connected to your body when you sing. That unconscious connection occurs because you sing from the abdomen. When monks chant, their song enables them to become completely present and fully conscious—and the vehicle to this place is the breath. Breath engages the conscious mind with unconscious intent. When you breathe from the abdomen, you are closer to nature.

Abdominal Breathing

Riding Goals: Relaxation, Awareness

The goal of this exercise is to be in constant control of your breath while mounted. Your goal is to move your breath into the abdomen, and in order to do so, your abdomen must become relaxed without sacrificing your structural alignment. When you relax, your lower back, pelvis, and spine will move freely within your center. In return, this freer movement deepens the seat and allows you to match the rhythm of the horse. Matching the horse's rhythm is another way of becoming one with your horse. When you ride in this way, your horse has to spend much less energy and focus balancing you on his back. When you match your horse, you allow him to move more freely and effectively in any gait.

Function

Abdominal breathing expands your thoracic cavity downward. The benefits of deep abdominal breathing are many. Here are a few—you'll discover more with time.

- Increased vital capacity of the heart and lungs

- Greater unity of mind and body

- Smoother, more rhythmic body motions

- Reduced stress, especially in the lower back and shoulders

- Deeper, natural relaxation and released tension

- Freer, unlocked energy centers (gates) within the body

- Fewer injuries

Intent

Use your mind to direct your breath down into your Dain Tian, and then locate and identify any tension in your body. Use your mind to "think in"—to direct or see with your mind the intended action of your body (or bodies, such as you and your horse) a moment prior to manifesting the physical action.

Step-by-Step

Unmounted

1. Begin in *Standing Meditation* so that you can enter the exercise from a quiet, centered place (p. 37).

2. Place your hands in front of your abdomen with your palms facing your body. Create a diamond shape with your fingers by placing the tips of the thumbs together and the tips of your index fingers together.

3. Place your thumbs on your belly button, and your palms against your abdomen.

4. Exhale completely while gently "sucking in" your stomach. Focus your mind on the space inside the diamond, and feel your hands against your belly.

Steps 2 and 3

5. Inhale, and use your mind to direct your breath down into the abdomen. You will feel your belly pushing out against your hands as you breathe in.

6. Exhale, and repeat. Try to take long, smooth, deep breaths. As you exhale, feel your stomach return to its relaxed state.

In the beginning, practice abdominal breathing for one minute at a time. As you become successful at expanding your abdomen by inhaling and filling your lungs completely, you may increase the time to suit your needs. Five minutes of abdominal breathing while in *Standing Meditation* is a wonderful way to release stress in your body and mind prior to riding.

The Simplicity and Power of Breath

The fluidity on horseback that you can achieve through abdominal breathing exemplifies all the Eight Principles we discussed earlier:

- Use the mind, not force
- Never oppose force with force
- Yield and overcome
- Balance like a scale
- Seek stillness in motion
- Be heavy and light
- Focus and expand
- Remember that art is long, life is short.

Western culture tends to value the complex. Breath is overlooked because of its apparent simplicity. Tai Chi understands the profound power of the simple.

Step 2

Step 4

Mounted

As you may have already discovered from your groundwork, retraining the way you breathe takes a great deal of focus and concentration. You have to be able to focus completely on your breath and body while you practice; you don't want to be distracted by your horse. Therefore, begin the exercise with your horse either in a round pen or on the longe line. Because horses react, sometimes strongly, to the rider's breath, you'll need a friend to direct your horse. Your hands will then be free of the reins and you'll be free to concentrate.

1 Begin in *Sitting Meditation* (p. 40).

2 Start at the walk (later you'll progress to the trot and canter). While walking on a 20-meter circle or the perimeter of a round pen, become aware of where your breath is in your body. Is it up in your chest or down in your belly? Your arms should

Step 9 and 10: Two views

hang at your sides. Allow the motion of the horse and gravity to lengthen your arms, and feel the weight of your arms pulling your shoulders down.

3 Form a "diamond" with your hands, just as you did in the unmounted portion of this exercise. Place your thumbs on your belly button with your palms lying against your abdomen.

4 Focus your mind on the space inside the "diamond." Use your mind to direct your breath down into your abdomen.

5 As you inhale, feel your belly push out against your hands. As you exhale, feel your stomach shrink away from your hands.

6 Repeat this exercise completing at least 3 circles.

When you're sitting well with your breath dropped down in your abdomen, the motion of your horse will often feel bigger and rounder. Your hips and upper body may now be moving more rhythmically.

James On Your Shoulder

Imagine your breath dropping down into your pelvic girdle and groin area. Feel these areas relax and expand. Your breath should be smooth and natural— don't force it. Think about allowing the motion of the horse to help move your breath down.

7 At this time briefly turn your attention to your horse. Do you feel that he is more relaxed and moving more freely underneath you? Your horse's breathing pattern may have changed, having become more regular and relaxed.

8 Change direction and practice this exercise making at least 3 circles in the new direction.

9 After you have had some success breathing into your belly, move your inside hand behind your back, placing the backside of the hand against your lower back (the Ming Meng). Your outside hand remains on your belly. Through your hands, feel whether or not your lower back expands as you breathe in. Remember that the abdomen can expand away from the center of the body in all directions just as a balloon can expand in all directions.

10 With your hands still in place—front and back—walk 2 complete circles. Feel the movement of your body.

Focus your mind on the area under your hand on your lower back. Imagine that area filling with air and becoming soft. In the beginning, it might help if you round your lower back to make room for the breath. Rounding the lower back can create freedom of movement in the lumbar area of the spine. Can you feel your spine being moved by the horse? Feel how the horse moves you. Can you feel the moments where you can move your seat without interfering with the rhythm of your horse?

You won't hold the position of rounding your back. To find your center, you must first define the outside edges, and this is an outside edge. The origins of this rounding come from the abdomen and lumbar, not the tailbone or seat. This is not tucking or pulling the tailbone under. Without the ability to move the lower spine independently of the rest of the spine, most riders will tuck the tailbone in an attempt to round or soften the lower back. You may want to return to *Wall Sitting* (p. 59) to help you develop a more independent motion of the lower lumbar spine.

11 When you are able to incorporate *Abdominal Breathing* successfully at the walk, try it at the trot and canter. Ideally, you will be working on a longe line so that your hands will be free to feel your body. If you are in a round pen and must hold the reins, alternate the hand holding the reins to free the other hand to feel your body.

Ah-Ha!

As you begin to drop your breath, you will feel more stable and relaxed. You will become more aware of unnecessary tension in the body and be able to release it as you exhale. Your mind will become clearer and your body will feel lighter.

Your Dain Tian is the home of your chi. A good belly laugh opens your Dain Tian, so ask a friend to tell you a good joke while you ride. When you laugh, you relax and don't try so hard to hold your position. Laugh on your horse, and it changes your seat.

I also recommend riding bareback at the walk. You can gain so much: a better sense of the horse's movement and rhythm; a better sense of your own movement and rhythm; and an ever-increasing general sense of confidence on horseback, coupled with an ever-diminishing sense of fear of riding or falling.

> *Rider Insight, Silke: Silke experienced severe back pain. When she rode her young Friesian stallion, she realized she was holding her spine rigid and tight. When she started focusing on her breathing, she was able to relax her lower back. She worked on breathing both on and off the horse. After she'd completed three sessions of breathing while mounted, she found her pain had disappeared.*

Ability Transition

Throughout the day, you will begin to catch yourself whenever you hold your breath. With a little experience, you will notice that this holding is always preceded by physical or emotional stress. As abdominal breathing becomes natural, you will find yourself thinking less and feeling more.

Reminder

Remember that you breathe in and out over 23,000 times a day. Your body may not be used to the larger amount of oxygen abdominal breathing supplies to your lungs, and it is common in the first days of practice to feel a bit light-headed or dizzy. Do not be alarmed, because your body will soon get used to the increased oxygen, and the light-headedness will disappear.

Many of my students, after having practiced a few days, have a breakthrough while lying in bed just before they fall asleep. Up until now, breathing for most of you has been an unconscious habit. Now I am asking you to make a conscious effort to change the manner in which you breathe. When you master abdominal breathing, you'll find it an exciting accomplishment and it will become an automatic function of your body. You'll no longer have to think about it, because it will happen naturally.

You may be concerned about keeping the appearance of a flat, hard stomach, even while breathing from the belly. The strength training to get those "abs" works your exterior muscles. You can make your muscles so taut that they won't expand, but to breathe from the abdomen, your muscles must be elastic so that they can relax. There is a balance that must be reached—hard flat abs that aren't flexible are the equivalent of being muscle-bound in the abdomen.

Counting Your Breath

Your horse hears your breath. When you are not in control of your breath, you are not in control of your horse. *Counting Your Breath* helps you gain control of your breath, which in turn creates your rhythm.

Function

Counting Your Breath increases your awareness of your own body and the horse's. You will find the rhythm of your breath, and the rhythm of your breath—its cadence—sets the rhythm of your body. When you are more connected to your own body and its natural rhythm, you allow the horse to find his own rhythm.

Intent

Counting the breath demands the complete attention of your mind on your body. This attention develops your focus and concentration.

Step-by-Step

Mounted

As with *Abdominal Breathing*, this exercise is most effective if done in a round pen or on a longe line. Ask a friend for assistance so that you can concentrate on the exercise while he or she directs your horse.

1 Begin in *Sitting Meditation.*

2 Start at the walk. For the first few minutes, just focus on your breath. Are you breathing from the abdomen? If not, allow yourself the time to drop your breath down to your belly.

3 Count the number of breaths you take on a complete circle. To keep things consistent, count one inhalation and the accompanying exhalation as one breath.

How many did you take? Say the number out loud to yourself or your longe partner.

4 Repeat the counting for 2 more circles. Did the number of breaths you took change? The more relaxed and connected you become with your body, the fewer breaths you will take on the circle.

5 Now you'll repeat the counting at the trot. As you ask for the trot, notice whether you are breathing in or out.

It is not the inhaling or exhaling that is important; it is your awareness that's important.

6 Count the number of breaths you take on a complete circle again, and say the number out loud to yourself or your longe partner. Notice how the rhythm of your breath changes at the trot in comparison to the walk.

Ah-Ha!

You will realize that you are breathing in rhythm with your motion.

Ability Transition

As you practice this exercise, you will be less prone to becoming distracted or losing track of the count, and the number of breaths you take will decrease as your lung capacity increases and breathing relaxes.

Reminder

Throughout this and all the breathing exercises, don't force a change in your breathing patterns. In the saddle, you should feel relaxed and calm. Allow your breath to drop lower into your belly.

Open the Ming Meng

Riding Goals: Relaxation, Awareness

Open the Ming Meng teaches you to let go of tension in your lower back through abdominal breathing.

Function

The exercise opens the Ming Meng, which relaxes and engages the lower lumbar region of your back, allowing your seat to move more freely with the horse. *Opening the Ming Meng* also allows the energy of the horse to move up through your seat into the rest of your body.

Intent

Use your mind to direct your breath into your lower back area. Expand and open the Ming Meng, inviting your horse's energy up.

Step-by-Step

Unmounted

Before starting this exercise, review *Wall Sitting* (p. 59). The practice of wall sitting introduces you to the physical motion of opening the Ming Meng. Combining that knowledge with your intent is the key to learning how to *Open the Ming Meng* while standing or riding your horse.

1 Begin in *Standing Meditation.*

2 Practice a few deep abdominal breaths to relax the belly. (Review, if necessary, *Abdominal Breathing,* p. 90.)

3 Slowly and completely exhale all the air from your lungs while you slightly "suck in" your gut.

4 Slowly begin to inhale into your abdomen, allowing your belly to expand. As your belly expands, move your intent to your lower back. While continuing to inhale, slightly round your lower back (the same motion as in *Wall Sitting*), and allow your

back to expand with your breath. It will feel as if your tailbone is dropping toward the ground.

You may find it helpful to imagine a weight attached by a string to your tailbone that helps pull it down. However, this visualization sometimes causes riders to try to force the tailbone to drop—this is not correct. Dropping of the tailbone is the *result* of expanding and moving the lumbar region, not the cause. During the mounted portion of this exercise it is impossible to move your tailbone down without causing a great deal of tension in your thighs and seat. On the other hand, moving the lumbar region with your intent is effortless and this is your goal.

5 Exhale and let your belly and back shrink and contract.

6 Repeat Steps 1 through 5 until your back expands freely with your breath and intent.

Mounted

You will do the mounted practice of this exercise at the walk. I suggest riding in a large arena so that you won't have to divert your attention to changing direction because you're running out of space. Riding along a straight trail also works well. If neither are available, that's okay—just be aware of the distractions that will pull your intent away from your body.

1 Begin in *Sitting Meditation*.

2 Walk forward and take a few deep abdominal breaths. Allow your belly to relax and expand with each inhalation.

3 Exhale completely and become aware of the sucking in of your belly. If the exhalation causes you to tense up in your back or abdomen, repeat Steps 2 and 3 until you are completely relaxed in your body while breathing.

4 As you inhale and your belly begins to expand, move your intent to your lower back (the Ming Meng). Use your intent and breath to allow the lower back to relax and expand.

Use your intent to combine the experience of *Wall Sitting* and the groundwork portion of this exercise. As your Ming Meng opens, you will feel more connection with the horse through your seat. You may experience some discomfort in your seat bones until they've become accustomed to staying in complete contact with the leather of the saddle.

When I first started riding and was experimenting with the opening of the Ming Meng, I experienced an innate fear of letting go with my lower back. Upon investigation I found this fear had nothing to do with my back, but it had to do with my front, with the anatomical differences between men and women. When any rider lets go and opens the Ming Meng there will be more contact, both front and back, with the saddle. For men this can occasionally produce great discomfort, particularly at the trot and canter. The first step in overcoming this problem is to purchase riding attire that provides maximum support. The second step is to continue to develop a more centered and secure seat, and all the exercises in this book will help you with that.

Ah-Ha!

You will begin to experience the sensation of your intent moving your breath in your body. You will feel the skin covering your lower back stretching with the expansion. Imagine the skin of a balloon stretching as it inflates.

Ability Transition

When your body has become familiar with this newfound movement, you will begin to be able to open the Ming Meng by simply willing it open. You will couple the experience and ability developed on the ground and direct it with your intent.

Reminder

Forcing the Ming Meng open is not possible, and trying to do so is very counterproductive. If you aren't successful, don't worry. Relax and review the groundwork, including *Counting Your Breath* (p. 97), to build a stronger foundation. Eventually your breath will fill your abdomen like water poured into a glass, the gathering energy filling you from the bottom up, not from the top down.

Embracing the Moon

Riding Goals: Position, Seat

Embracing the Moon will teach you to train your breath to move down into the abdomen while keeping your upper body relaxed, engaged, and open. This form allows the horse more freedom of motion in his front end. It puts your upper body, arms, and wrists into the optimum alignment for holding the reins, and it creates a higher awareness and sensitivity in your hands.

Function

This exercise teaches you to use your arms, chest, and upper back in a more balanced and effective manner, while developing consistent abdominal breathing. It keeps you from bracing with your chest.

Intent

You'll envision a large sphere embraced within your arms. Imagine that your arms are supported by and held round by the sphere. With every breath, your arms become lighter and rounder. After learning the exercise's movements, focus your mind on the area inside the sphere within your arms. Imagine your breath filling the sphere and expanding it until it encompasses your whole body.

Step-by-Step

Unmounted

1 Begin in *Standing Meditation.*

2 Next perform *Sink and Circulate the Chi* (p. 51). Remember to breathe from the abdomen.

3 Slowly lift your arms out to your sides. Bring your hands to shoulder level, keeping your thumbs up and your palms facing forward. Pause and imagine that you are about to hug a loved one. Your arms should be slightly bent at the elbows. Think wrapping, not grabbing!

Steps 1 and 2   *Step 3*

Steps 4 and 5: Two views

4 Circle your still-bent arms to the front of your body until your hands are approximately two fists apart, at shoulder level. As your arms sweep forward, rotate your wrists so that by the time your hands come near each other, your thumbs are now pointed down and your palms facing forward. Feel this motion originating in your back, not your shoulders.

5 Pause in this position and complete 2 or 3 cycles of abdominal breathing.

6 Slowly lower your hands back to your sides, following the same path in which you raised them.

Mounted

The exercise works best when practiced on a longe line or in a round pen. Ask a friend for assistance so that you can concentrate on the exercise while he or she directs your horse.

1 Repeat the same motions and breathing patterns in the saddle as you did on the ground. Note that the photographs show a slightly more advanced version of the exercise; the hands have been brought to the front with the palms facing the rider. Some people find it easier to open their backs in this version, but you must also be careful to keep your shoulders completely relaxed.

2 Practice for at least 2 full circles.

3 After you have completed the circles, let your elbows drop slowly to your sides and let your hands drop softly as if holding the reins.

Ah-Ha!

The front of your chest will be soft and your upper back will feel expanded. You may feel a sensation like heat or pins and needles in your hands.

Ability Transition

As you become familiar with the motions, explore the rotation of your arms within the larger motion of the embrace. The rotation helps keep tension from finding a home in your shoulders and neck.

You will notice that your breath begins to fill your body from the belly up. With time, your breath will expand your lower back and then move up to fill your upper back, where it will open Gate 4: The Back of the Heart. When the mind and body connect through these motions, the Front and Back of the Heart gates are opened.

Learn to open Gate 3: The Front of your Heart by imagining how you hug someone. It may not be easy for you to open the Front of the Heart, because in riding, you protect your front. Think about the feeling of drawing back the string of a bow; do this on both sides of your body. Let go of the muscles.

Drop your sternum. Let your breath travel down to your abdomen, then back, and up, and around your upper back. Visualize a circle opening and expanding. You don't expand your heart up and out as though inhaling strongly, like a soldier sucking in a big breath when coming to attention. This is expansion through relaxation. You cannot use force.

Think of opening your Dain Tian, Ming Meng, and Back of the Heart gates as a progression. You might imagine a series of circles painted on your skin; now expand each circle, one after the other.

Reminder

Let the rhythm of your horse at the walk help slow and deepen your breath. Don't force the movement of your breath, but direct it with your mind. Pay close attention to your shoulders, and do not hold the position so long that you create tension in them. Think of the breath filling your abdomen as supporting your shoulders.

Step 1: Two views

Heaven and Earth

Riding Goals: Relaxation, Awareness

Heaven and Earth teaches you to breathe from your abdomen in a rhythmic manner while moving your arms and eyes. When done in the saddle, this exercise aids in relaxing you and your horse.

Function

The exercise develops your ability to control and manipulate the breath to maintain balance and rhythm while in the saddle.

Intent

Use your mind to direct the movement of your breath within your body. As you look upward and your palms face the heavens, imagine that your arms reach out and embrace the heavens. As you scoop down, imagine that your hands go deep into the ground and pull the energy of the earth into your body. You may then release the energy up into the heavens as you raise your arms again. As my teacher would say, "We become the bridge that joins heaven and earth."

Also observe with your mind the changes in your horse as your breath relaxes and becomes deeper and more rhythmic.

Step-by-Step

Unmounted

The general rule for breathing in this exercise is that when your arms are moving up or out, you breathe in; when your arms are moving down or in, you breathe out. The objective is to create an even rhythm of breathing in which to explore the possibilities of expanding and contracting the body from the inside out.

Your breath should be soft and smooth, never held or forced. Your breath should set the pace of the exercise.

1 Begin in *Standing Meditation.*

Step 3 *Step 4*

2 From *Standing Meditation*, you may push your heels out by pivoting on the balls of your feet so that your feet are slightly pigeon-toed (not shown in these photos). This position helps relax the muscles of your lower back.

3 Raise both hands in front of you until arms are shoulder level, with your elbows slightly bent and your palms facing downward.

There is a rotation of your arms that causes your palms to face down. The rotation is created from the shoulder, not the elbow.

During the entire *Heaven and Earth* exercise, your head and eyes follow your hands. As you move your head, be sure to use only your neck, and not your upper back.

4 Circle your arms out to the sides and down in an arcing motion. Continue the movement until your hands are in front of your Dain Tian (at your waist) with the palms facing upward. Your fingertips should point at each other and be approximately 6 inches apart.

Step 5

Step 6

Step 7

5 Slowly raise your hands, palms up, toward your chest, maintaining the distance between them.

6 As your hands pass in front of your face, rotate your hands outward and continue raising your arms, pushing your palms, now facing up, sending energy toward the sky (Heaven). Follow your hands aloft with your eyes.

7 Release your arms and let them arc down. Relax your shoulders, your arms, and your hands. Let them travel down and return to your Dain Tian in a scooping motion, with the palms facing up (having gathered energy from Earth).

8 Repeat Steps 4, 5, and 6 for a total of 3 repetitions. On the last repetition, let your hands drop to your sides.

Mounted

Practice this exercise while riding at the walk on a loose rein or longe line. Ask a friend for assistance so that you can concentrate on the exercise while he or she directs your horse.

Ah-Ha!

You will notice that both your belly and lower back expand with your inhalation. You will feel your shoulders relax as your arms rotate.

While in the saddle, you may observe that your horse stops walking when your head begins to move. When this happens, it is most likely because your seat has tightened slightly and stopped moving with the horse. Consider this response a good thing, because it proves how easily you're distracted from your seat and how a subtle change in your body affects your horse. Learn how to change this in Ability Transition next.

Ability Transition

As you practice *Heaven and Earth*, you will notice that your motions seem to become bigger and rounder. This change happens when the muscles in your chest and arms begin to relax while in motion. The rotation of the arms plays a vital role in the relaxation of the entire body.

Performing the steps for Heaven and Earth while mounted.

Reminder

While you practice, search your body for tension and then ask yourself what the cause is. Is it because you lost your balance and are now working to hold yourself in position? Or is the tension there in the form of an old habit? In either case, search within the form for the moment that the tension is born. When you find it, you can then discover the root cause of your tension and retrain yourself—preventing the tension from reappearing in your body.

Remember that you start the *unmounted* phase of every exercise from *Standing Meditation*, in complete relaxation and balance. And you start the *mounted* phase of every exercise from *Sitting Meditation*, again, in complete relaxation and balance. You want to maintain this balance throughout the form and throughout your ride. To constantly be letting go of tension is not true balance. Discovering, changing, and flowing through the moments when tension is born—*before it takes hold*—is true balance and the essence of Tai Chi.

Breathing to a Halt or Walk

Riding Goals: Rhythm, Awareness, Influencing the Horse

This exercise teaches you that your horse listens to your breath. You can use your breath to slow the motion of your pelvis and communicate a halt to the horse.

Function

You move your center forward, so your weight drops into your seat bones. This exercise also helps you in the half-halt, where you communicate to get the horse's attention. Your breath is a convincing aid. By using your breath, you will only need to give one-quarter of the aid that you previously gave to get a halt.

Intent

Think about sitting down to get the halt. Look at the ground 20 feet in front of you, and imagine that you bring the ground straight up into a wall in front of you. Raise the ground like a drawbridge.

Step-by-Step

Unmounted

1 Begin in *Standing Meditation*.

2 Sit down in a chair and practice abdominal breathing.

3 Fill your abdomen with air, and expand it forward. That feeling will be your halt. With abdominal breathing, your center shifts forward when you inhale. In riding, this means that your center shifts forward so more weight drops into the front of your seat bones. This change is very subtle and can hardly be seen from the outside of the body. You're experiencing a physical change of your center.

4 Exhale and sense your center shifting backward.

Mounted

1 Begin in *Sitting Meditation.*

2 Walk your horse on a straight line.

3 Breathe into and expand your Dain Tian forward. As you expand your belly, you drop more of your weight to the front of your seat bones. This slows the movement in your pelvis, signaling your horse to halt.

Feel the influence your breath has on the motion of your pelvis.

Ah-Ha!

You will notice with practice that your horse begins to halt as soon as you start your inhale. When you use your breath, your horse listens. When you exhale, more weight drops into the back of your seat bones—use this reaction as a driving aid.

Ability Transition

Remember that though your horse may be big, he is sensitive. Drop your weight to the front of the saddle by ounces, not by pounds. Abdominal breathing changes the volume of your center. In changing the volume, you change the distribution of weight over your seat bones. This slight weight shift directed by your breath is a powerful yet subtle tool.

Reminder

Many riders fail to drop the weight to the front of the saddle. They bring their energy (breath) up into the chest, so that the chest—not the center—becomes the root of the halt. Then, when they pull the reins to halt, the horse resists and pulls the rider's seat bones up. The result is the opposite of sitting down to stop. Remember, too, that your horse is also learning. It will take time and practice for both of you to get used to this new communication.

A Culture of Harmony

When I ask riders, "Where is your breath," many don't know. Everything in the universe is controlled by an underlying rhythm. In riding, rhythm is the key to timing. Now that you're mindful of your breath's timing, you've started to tune in to your horse's breathing as well. Your breath can harmonize with your horse's breath, so the two of you can truly join centers.

The horse has a rhythm to his breathing. Look for your horse's breath. His breathing will communicate his physical and mental state, so you can sense his attitude moment by moment.

Horses are sensitive to our breathing. Over the years I have found that when I breathe, the horse breathes. The first few times it happened I thought it was a coincidence, but with time I've found it happens too regularly to be just a coincidence. I have also found that when the rider exhales and relaxes, the horse exhales and relaxes, too.

You can control the rhythm of your breath to match your horse's rhythm. Start by enhancing your perception of how your horse breathes. From the ground, observe how he inhales and exhales at rest and at the walk.

From the saddle, pay attention to his breathing at the trot. At the canter, your horse will take bigger breaths and exhale more loudly. You'll notice that he breathes in rhythm with his stride. Listen to the rhythm of the horse's breath at the canter; it should be smooth and rhythmic.

Summary

All these exercises introduced you to the power of breathing. It's natural not to think about breathing all the time. Once you've retrained your breath, you can forget about it because you will have created a new awareness and positive habits of breathing.

There's a Taoist saying, "Work is done, then forgotten. Therefore it lasts forever." All this breath training is a means to an end. The end is to have breathing become unconscious and correct. Breathing is a powerful tool to be used consciously when necessary and one that never unconsciously works against you. Tai Chi examines the ways of nature in order to become closer to it. Babies breathe correctly, and they don't think about it. A newborn colt knows how to walk, trot, and canter, and he doesn't think about it. That's what I want you to do—think less, feel more, and always know where your breath is.

What's Next

In chapter 6, "Your Body: Enhancing Your Movement and Power," we will work with a set of nine more Laing Gong exercises in order to develop enhanced mobility.

6

Your Body

Enhancing Your Movement and Power

THERE IS A FANTASTIC SYNERGY that can occur between mind, breath, and body. Having focused on mind and breath in earlier chapters, now we will focus on body, in concert with mind and breath.

The goal of this chapter is to train your body to move in a new way, from the inside out. We will use your innate physical abilities to relax and to be aware of your body and couple them with exercises that expand your range of motion and develop your strength. From this training you will gain "enhanced mobility."

Enhanced Mobility

Enhanced mobility is the ability to move

a) through an increased range of motion,

b) with greater control and strength, and

c) with your abdomen and back in relaxed, structural alignment.

Enhanced mobility is based upon *internal* strength (mind, breath, alignment, and balance), not *external* strength (muscles acting in isolation). All the exercises in this chapter work to help you develop enhanced mobility that will assist you as you negotiate the forces at play when riding.

There are three sets of forces in action when you ride: those developed by the horse (his momentum); those transferred from the horse to you (your momentum); and those within your body (your own muscular effort). Of these, you only have control of the last. By developing enhanced mobility, you are better able to move any part of your body without being overwhelmed by the greater force of the horse or by your own momentum. Enhanced mobility optimizes your ability to remain connected to your horse *and* to move independently of him. Paradoxically, only when you can remain independent of your horse, can you really join centers with him. Learning to ride in this way is an unending process because you and your horse must find your center again every time you ride.

Balance without Force

When you ride, you are dealing with a force bigger and stronger than you. You must learn to deal with the horse's potentially unbalancing movement. If you rely on strength, you're using your force to try to oppose the force of the horse. This approach has three problems: (1) the horse is far stronger than you; (2) using force inhibits a joint's flexibility; (3) using force produces injuries. In the course of your life, you may only oppose bigger stronger forces with force for so long before your body begins to pay the price.

Up until now I've talked about mind-body unity and moving the body as a whole. When you are training for enhanced mobility, you isolate a joint and a muscle group and discover how to use less muscular effort to get more effective motion by applying the principles of Tai Chi.

Root Causes

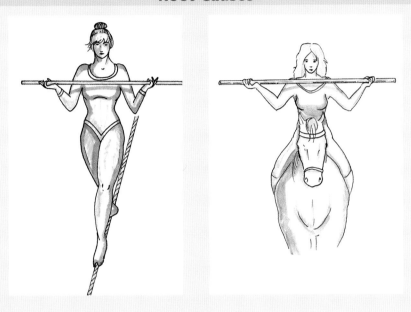

Riders often mistake the symptom of a problem as its cause, and then they treat only the symptom. In doing so, you may alter the symptom, but your cure will be ineffective because the root cause will remain unchanged. If you discover a specific physical problem, examine its root. Investigate and dig for the internal cause of an external symptom. What is your body telling you?

For example, the "elbows out" position (a symptom) can be the consequence of being immobile in your spine (root cause). This immobility means that you cannot absorb the horse's motion and you are thrown out of balance, which causes more tension and rigidity. You bring your elbows out to your sides to help yourself regain your balance, much as a tightrope walker holds a long pole for balance. Telling yourself to drop your elbows is no more helpful than telling the tightrope walker to drop her balance pole. In reality, you both need to make proactive, internal (root) adjustments that will enhance your balance.

Enhanced Mobility Training: Laing Gong

This chapter's nine exercises are all derived from *Laing Gong*, the set of therapeutic exercises introduced in chapter 4. The ultimate goal of these exercises is to train your body's muscles to work together, so your body moves as one—a cohesive unit of mind-body, muscle-bone, and inside-outside. In order to accomplish this complex and ambitious aim, I will break down the training into more easily learned exercises. The first three exercises address the neck and shoulders; the last six address the back, pelvis, and spine.

Please note that these exercises should always be performed while standing; their mechanics require you to stand and support your body against gravity using your bones instead of muscular effort. Of course, the mounted adaptations of these exercises are performed sitting—but you are still supporting yourself as you sit in the sort of self-carriage you learned in *Sitting Meditation* (p. 40).

Neck Turns

Riding Goals: Position/Seat, Relaxation

An enhanced awareness of balance is the first step in becoming truly aligned with the horse. You'll improve your posture and seat, and relax your body to relax the horse. The goal is to keep your head in balance over your shoulders and torso without causing undue tension in your neck and shoulder muscles.

Function

Neck Turns develops truly independent use of your head and neck. You'll be able to move your head and neck in a relaxed manner, without engaging any other muscle in your body. The exercise also helps to release tension in your neck and shoulders.

Intent

Imagine that the crown of your head is suspended from above and your whole body is as light as a feather. The more you turn your head, the taller you become. Visualize the smallest muscles in your neck moving your head, as the larger ones relax and allow your head to turn without restriction.

Step-by-Step

Unmounted

1 Begin in *Standing Meditation* (p. 37).

2 Place your hands on your hips, with your fingers pointing forward. Your legs are straight, not locked and not bent.

3 Slowly turn your head to the left, making sure it stays level as you turn. Don't look down or up. This is the first movement of the 4-part movement in which you'll turn your head left, right, up, and down.

4 When you feel you are at the end of your range of motion, stretch a little farther for just one second. Remember to keep your head straight. Don't sacrifice the position of your head to stretch further. Lock your knees and straighten your body during the one-second stretch period; do this for each of the 4 directions you'll turn.

Step 2

Step 3

5 Release the tension and return to the center—that is, the starting position, with your head over your body in relaxed natural alignment.

6 Turn your head to the right and stretch for one second, remembering to keep your head straight, then return to the center. Remember to lock your knees and straighten your body during the one-second stretch period.

7 Lift your chin to the sky as you stretch for one second, and then return to the center.

Be sure you don't arch your back while lifting your head. You should lift your chin rather than tilt your head back. By focusing on lifting the chin, you exercise the highest vertebra in your neck. Control of this area is essential for true balance.

8 Bring your chin down to your chest, stretch for one second, and return to the starting position.

9 Repeat the exercise 4 times.

Step 6

Step 7

Step 8

Mounted

Practice *Neck Turns* while riding at the walk on a loose rein or longe line. Ask a friend for assistance so that you can concentrate on the exercise while he or she directs your horse. A partner is also helpful in giving you feedback on the correctness of your position, which often varies from what you think and feel.

You may want to start this exercise at the halt, and then work at the walk. After you are comfortable with it at the walk, move into the trot and canter. The steps are the same for the mounted work as they are for the groundwork. Keep these thoughts in mind as you work:

- While turning your head, avoid tightening the muscles in your neck. Tightening them will interfere with the balance of your head over your body, which will in turn cause you to tense in order to balance yourself. Such tension will decrease the fluid movement of your spine, and your horse may stop or move poorly—not the desired result, but certainly useful feedback from your equine partner.
- When you stretch your chin to the sky, imagine that you are stretching upward and slightly forward. Otherwise you may find yourself slightly behind your center and the movement of your horse. If you fall behind the motion, your lower back will tighten and drop more weight into the back of your seat, which can cause your horse to accelerate. Falling behind can also create a tremendous amount of stress in your lower back.
- When stretching the chin to the chest pay attention not to lean forward as your chin and eyes go down. If you do, your horse may let you know by coming to a halt.

Ah Ha!

Notice how much your balance depends on where you are looking. Soon you will be able to look away and remain completely aware of your center. This exercise is great for increasing your awareness of the overall rhythm of your body and how the smallest unbalanced movement can completely alter that rhythm.

You should feel as if your head can rotate on an axis. Your shoulders will not rise, and you will feel an even stretch on both sides of the neck with no "kinks." You may experience a tingling sensation up the back of your neck and over the top of your head, as you open and expand your crown.

Performing Neck Turns while mounted

Ability Transition

With practice you will significantly increase the range of motion of your head and neck. You will also begin to catch yourself holding your head in a poor position at different times during the day, and you'll be able to realign and relax your head and neck before tension sets in.

Reminder

Remember to hold the stretch for only one second. Holding it longer does not increase the benefit. The goal in all these exercises is to develop a slow, even, balanced motion with a complete awareness of your body. Take your time; don't hurry. There are no shortcuts to achieving good results.

Make sure you are completely balanced throughout the exercise at the walk before trying it at the trot.

Use this as a mounted warm-up every time you ride. You will be amazed how much more you'll get out of your training if you take the time to warm up first.

Spread Your Chest

Riding Goals: Position/Seat, Rhythm, Influencing the Horse

Spread Your Chest develops the enhanced mobility of your shoulders and chest necessary for increasing the sensitivity of your hands. It helps soften your chest, shoulders, and upper back. And finally, the exercise will help you maintain the rhythm of your seat and your connection with the horse.

The mounted version of this exercise enhances your ability to balance your upper body. It also teaches you to recognize and release tension in your arms, chest, and shoulders.

Function

Spreading your chest teaches you to move energy through your neck and shoulders down the back and into your seat; this helps you keep your upper body free from the tension that leads to fatigue. It can also help prevent chronic injuries of the neck and shoulders.

You may experience some popping or cracking noises in your shoulder joints. Don't be alarmed—it is natural for the body to make noise as the muscles, tendons, and ligaments stretch, realign, and heal. However, if you have had any shoulder injuries, you must use caution in doing this exercise. You may experience some discomfort in the shoulder while performing the stretch, but it should not be painful. Only you can determine the difference between discomfort and pain. In any case, you should feel no pain after completing the exercise. Often we have to move through and past discomfort in order to heal an old injury.

The position and alignment of your bones during all the Laing Gong exercises is of vital importance. Only with proper position can you realize the tremendous healing nature of these exercises.

Intent

Imagine that your arms are stretching out from your spine, not just from your shoulders. Feel a sensation of heat moving out of your arms—use your mind to push heat out to your hands and then out beyond your fingertips.

As you become familiar with the motion, look at one hand, but focus your mind on the other; this concentration will engage both hemispheres of your brain simultaneously and increase awareness.

Steps 2 and 3   Step 4

Step-by-Step

Unmounted

1 Begin in *Standing Meditation.*

2 Stretch your arms straight down in front of your body, with your right palm on top of the back of the left hand. Lock your elbows; they remain locked throughout the exercise. Remember to hold your fingers together and thumbs out.

3 Your eyes and head look down at your right hand.

4 Raise your paired arms straight forward and up, until they are directly over your head. Keep your eyes on your right hand.

Steps 6, 7, and 8

Step 9

5 Stretch your arms up by bringing your shoulders to your ears for one second as you extend your fingers toward the sky.

6 Move your arms back past your head as you separate your hands, and push your arms out and back in a circular motion.

7 Keep your palms facing up by rotating the upper arm, not the forearm.

8 Follow your right hand with your eyes and head.

9 Continue to move your arms in a circular motion—back, out, and down. As your hands drop below the level of your shoulders, let the upper arm rotate forward while the arms return to the beginning position, but now with the left hand on top.

10 Repeat for your left side.

11 Once to the right and once to the left form one complete repetition. Do at least 4 repetitions.

Mounted

Practice *Spread Your Chest* while riding at the walk on a loose rein or longe line. Ask a friend for assistance.

1 Begin in *Sitting Meditation* (p. 40).

2 Riding at the walk, begin the exercise just as you would on the ground.

Notice how your body reacts to the movement of the horse as you begin to circle your arms back and out. Remember to keep your eyes on one hand—first on one side, and then on the other as you repeat the movement.

This form can create strong sensations in your arms and hands. You may feel a tingling or heat. It's not uncommon to experience a feeling of electricity shooting through your arms.

While mounted, you may even experience a feeling I can only describe as riding with an open heart—it will feel as if your horse's energy moves up through your body into your heart.

Physically, when the muscles of your chest and shoulders are relaxed, they soften and allow your spine to move more freely, and this enables you to maintain the alignment of your upper body over your center.

Ability Transition

When you gain control and flexibility in your neck and shoulders, the sensation of heat will subside and so should any "noise" in your shoulders. While you continue to practice on and off the horse, you will notice that your arms and shoulders will be more relaxed. You will feel the horse's mouth through your arms and chest, not just with your hands. With time, you'll feel your horse's mouth in your whole upper body. You'll monitor and control this connection using the Back of the Heart gate.

Reminder

As always, move softly, and gently keep your eyes on your hand throughout the form. Pay close attention to your back. It should be straight, not arched. Arching your back

Performing Spread Your Chest while mounted

in this exercise inhibits the range of motion of your shoulders and takes you out of structural alignment. Arching creates the illusion of flexibility in the shoulders by moving the whole chest and shoulder. Remember that the goal is a smooth, correct, controlled motion.

Spread Your Wings

Riding Goals: Balance, Rhythm

Spread Your Wings develops enhanced mobility in your shoulders and neck, which will enable you to keep your head balanced without undue tension. When your head is balanced, you allow the horse to move with more freedom. By opening your shoulder joints and the accompanying meridians, you will increase the sensitivity of your hands and fingers—helping you improve your communication with your horse.

Function

You'll develop the ability to move your arms and shoulders with minimal use of your upper trapezius muscles. You will also use your latissimus dorsi muscles to hold your shoulders down. (For anatomical references, see the *Appendix*, p. 245.) This independent movement allows your shoulders and energy to stay down, so you don't raise your center of gravity while raising your arms. This exercise also helps you learn to use your upper body while keeping your seat. A good seat is vital to maintaining the circuit that brings energy from the earth, up through the horse, into your seat, up through your body and out the reins to the horse, where it travels back down to the earth to begin the cycle again.

Intent

Focus your eyes and mind on your elbows. Imagine stretching your elbows out and away from your body while drawing large circles in the air with your elbows. As you become familiar with the motion, look at one elbow but focus your mind on the other. This focus will engage both hemispheres of your brain simultaneously and increase your awareness.

Step-by-Step

Unmounted

1 Begin in *Standing Meditation.*

This motion is much easier
to master on the ground
than in the saddle, so
develop your skills doing
the unmounted version
before doing the exercise
mounted.

2 Place your hands on your hips with your thumbs forward. Turn your head and look at your right elbow, as I am in the photo. Pull your elbows back and up, stretching the front of your chest open, while keeping your shoulders down and your palms close at your sides. Your eyes and head continue to follow the position of your right elbow.

3 Continue to lift your elbows back and up until they are higher than your shoulders. Keep your palms close to your body as your bent arms continue circling up. Circle your elbows toward the front of your body, allowing your hands to rise up to and through your armpits to the front of your chest.

4 The backs of your palms are now facing each other. Your wrists and fingers should be soft and relaxed. Your elbows should be higher than your wrists and your shoulders (trapezius muscles) should be relaxed and down.

Remember to follow the path of your right elbow with your eyes, but to keep your attention on the left elbow.

5 Using your wrist as a pivot point, allow your elbows to drop down and your palms to face forward—but not quite straight forward: your hands should be positioned as though you were holding a large ball in front of your face.

6 Relax your shoulders and elbows, while you allow your arms to return to the beginning position.

7 Repeat and focus this time on your left elbow.

8 Once to the right and once to the left form one complete repetition. Do at least 4 repetitions.

Mounted

The mounted version of *Spread Your Wings* is the virtually the same as the ground version. Practice it while riding at the walk on a loose rein or longe line. Ask a friend for assistance.

1 Begin in *Sitting Meditation.*

2 Do the exercise at the walk. Pay close attention to your seat while rotating your elbows. You will know immediately if you tighten the trapezius muscles because

Step 1

Step 2

Step 3

Step 4

Step 5

Performing Spread Your Wings while mounted, various views

your seat will tighten and you'll start to lose your balance backward and brace your lower back.

Have a friend watch the arm you are not looking at. Ask her to make sure that the motion of both your arms is the same.

Ah-Ha!

You should feel no tension in your neck or hands. The motion will become smooth and relaxed throughout. With practice, you will recognize the moment you engage unnecessary muscles in your shoulders and neck, and you'll be able to release them before they affect your balance or your connection with your horse.

Ability Transition

At some point you will learn to lift your elbows without raising your shoulders and creating any unnecessary tension that restricts motion. Your armpits will feel "empty," or completely without tension. While riding, this new ability will allow your head to move freely in rhythm with the horse, rather than requiring you to hold your head in place by tightening the muscles of your neck and shoulders. The exercise will also help you keep your shoulders and elbows down and relaxed.

Let me remind you of a story I mentioned earlier, as now you're doing an exercise that can help you achieve similar results. I studied a videotape of Olympic Gold Medalist Klaus Balkenhol's winning dressage test. At one point he cantered away from the camera down the centerline, giving you a perfect view of his back. His shoulders and spine seemed to be detached from one another. His spine moved up and down with the motion of the horse, but his shoulders remained still. This independent motion can only happen when the upper back and shoulders are completely relaxed and the spine is aligned naturally.

Interesting, too, was Balkenhol's overall profile: from the side, his posture looked more like that of a boxer, with the upper back full and slightly more rounded than the rigidly held, upright position I often see in even very accomplished riders. The tape showed a rider with all his gates open, moving in harmony with his horse and enjoying a beautiful ride.

Reminder

Move softly and gently. Breathe as you move, and support your elbows from below rather than lifting them with the trapezius muscles. Remember that any tension in your arms will show up in your hands. Think about keeping your armpits empty.

The Biomechanics of a Laing Gong Exercise

For riders interested in the biomechanics of Laing Gong, let's take a look at *Spread Your Chest* (p. 126).

There are six possible muscle actions involved in your upper limbs and shoulder joints:

1 Adduction

2 Abduction

3 Extension

4 Flexion

5 Medial rotation

6 Lateral rotation

Spread Your Chest includes all six motions. One muscle or group of muscles begins the motion, and then these muscles surrender to another group for the next part of the motion; this muscle group, in turn, surrenders to a following group, and so on, until the motion is completed. We often get energetically trapped in a motion by dominant muscles that can't let go sufficiently to allow the smaller, more sensitive muscles to take over.

In *Spread Your Chest*, for example, you need to use your trapezius to lift your shoulder blades, and the pectorals and deltoids to raise your arms. At some point you let go of the trapezius while continuing to use the pectorals. At some point above the height of your shoulder, the pectorals have to let go to allow the deltoids to take over the motion. To continue into the rotation back, the trapezius muscles need to relax again to allow the rhomboids to take over. The rhomboids then move the shoulder blades back, bringing along with them your shoulders and arms (see diagram on p. 247).

Hold the Sky with Both Hands

Riding Goals: Balance, Awareness, Position/Seat

Hold the Sky with Both Hands teaches you an effective way to transfer weight from one side of your seat to the other without creating tightness. When you ride with an aligned and evenly weighted seat, you often solve the problem of the horse's shoulders popping out or falling in while riding through a turn. The exercise can also be helpful in keeping the horse's haunches in line. Last, it is one of the best exercises I know for stretching and developing balance muscles in your lower back.

Function

You further develop your understanding of your body alignment and balance. You increase the flexibility of your lower lumbar vertebrae, abdomen, and waist, while maintaining structural balance. In the exercise, you shift weight into one or the other seat bone, while creating no tension in your seat or legs. When you lean to one side and maintain a straight spine the movement originates in the lower lumbar.

Intent

While performing this exercise, imagine your spine being completely fused together except for the last two vertebrae just above your pelvis. Use your mind not only to direct the lean but also to listen to what your muscles around your spine are saying.

Step-by-Step

Unmounted

1 Begin in *Standing Meditation.*

2 Lace your fingers together, palms down in front of your body. You are in the center position for the exercise. Look down at your hands.

3 Raise your hands up directly over your head, with your elbows locked. Swing your palms from facing down, to facing forward, to facing up. Stretch your hands to the sky by bringing your shoulders to your ears.

Step 2

Step 3

Step 4

Step 6

4 Lean to the left, while keeping your spine straight. Drop your breath deep into your abdomen before you start the lean. Exhale slowly as you lean.

Your head should travel only 2 to 6 inches to the side. Focus on doing the motion well, not in trying to lean as far as you can.

Focus your intent through your palms, which should be stretching upward through the whole exercise. Keep your shoulders to your ears during the lean.

The bend should come from as low as possible in your spine. Be sure to keep your hips stationary and your spine straight. You should feel this stretch in your lower back and hips.

Listen to the muscles in your lower back. Did they tighten without the consent of your mind? If so, direct them with your mind to relax.

5 Return to center position.

6 Repeat the exercise, this time leaning to the right.

7 Once to the left and once to the right form one complete repetition. Do at least 4 repetitions.

Mounted

Practice *Hold the Sky with Both Hands* first at the halt and then at the walk while on a loose rein or longe line. Ask a friend for assistance.

1 Begin in *Sitting Meditation.*

2 Repeat the unmounted Steps 2 through 6 while mounted.

The leaning movement is especially subtle when mounted; you need only lean far enough to move your head approximately one to 2 inches to the side (versus 2 to 6 inches when unmounted). Experiment and see how much you can accomplish moving your nose only one-half inch to the side.

The shift of weight created by your lean may cause your horse to adjust his stride to maintain balance. If you are leaning to the inside of the circle, your shift should make it easier for your horse to turn. However, if you lean to the outside of the circle, you may challenge your horse's balance because you're sending your horse a mixed message: your intent is telling your horse to ride on a circle; your seat bones are telling him to turn out of that circle. This is why it's best in the beginning to do this exercise from the halt. Refer back to the Riding Goals on page 138.

Performing Hold the Sky with Both Hands while mounted

Ah-Ha!

Feel as if you are moving your spine as a whole, with the motion originating in your lower lumbar vertebrae. While unmounted, as you practice you will find that with very little lean, you will feel a greater and greater shift of weight in your feet. You will slowly develop control of the smallest muscles in your back. They may feel a little sore after practice in the beginning. This is natural and is a good thing.

Ability Transition

Your goal is to have your bend come entirely from your lower lumbar vertebrae.

The sensitivity and strength of your seat lie in your lower back and abdomen, which are both enhanced by this exercise. When you gain control over these areas, you will be able to give aids using less effort and your horse will respond sooner, bringing you another step closer to your goal of riding with greater effectiveness. This is also in keeping with the first Principle: *Use the mind, not force* (see p. 16).

Hip Circles

Hip Circles develops strength and sensitivity in your hips (pelvis). Moving your hips enables you to follow the lateral motion of the horse's hindquarters without surrendering the structural alignment of your upper body.

You receive the force created by your horse through your seat, and your pelvis is the primary director of that force through your own body. If, from lack of flexibility, you do not direct this force effectively, it pushes you out of center (the combined center of you and your horse). When this happens, your horse must compensate, and his movement is inhibited. You may be unaware of your own role in your horse's diminished performance.

Function

Your pelvis lies at the center of your body. When it is tight and inflexible, the rest of your body must compensate for this lack of motion in ways that sometimes cause injuries, most often to the back, knees, and ankles. This exercise develops enhanced mobility in the pelvis, hip joints, and the lower lumbar vertebrae. It is an excellent form for healing back injuries.

Intent

Use your mind to keep your spine straight during the motions. Listen for unnecessary tension in your body.

Step-by-Step

Unmounted

1 Begin in *Standing Meditation* and place your hands on your hips, with your thumbs forward.

2 Push your hips out to the right, while keeping your spine and your legs straight. This is the first step in the diamond pattern in which you'll be moving your hips.

Step 3   *Step 4*   *Step 5*

3 Push your hips forward while supporting your upper body with your hands. Your hands help keep your spine straight.

4 Push to the left side while maintaining your structural alignment, still supporting your upper body with your hands.

5 Push your hips backward while keeping your head, neck, and spine in a straight line.

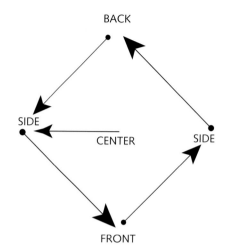

Step 6: Diamond Pattern of Hip Circles

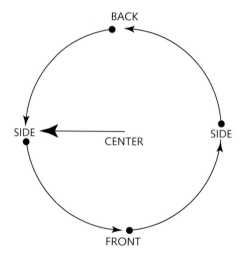

Step 7: Circular Pattern of Hip Circles

6 Move your hips in the diamond pattern one more time, completing 2 repetitions.

7 Move your hips in a circular pattern for the last 2 repetitions.

Ah-Ha!

When done correctly you will feel no tension in the lower back. Also, you will be able to maintain deep abdominal breathing throughout the exercise.

Ability Transition

As with all these exercises, the feelings you have in your body will change with time and practice. You might first feel the stretch in your hip on the side you are pushing toward. In time, the stretch may move up into your rib area or down into your thigh.

Enhanced mobility in the pelvis will help your riding. You will be more flexible and move in greater balance. As a result, you will need less time to warm up, and you'll find you have more energy—as will your horse, because he will be spending less energy compensating for your stiffness and imbalance.

Reminder

Be sure to move your hips out from under your upper body, rather than just leaning to the side, front, and back with your upper body. When done correctly, if you look down during the stretch, you should see that a line dropped straight down from your nose never falls outside your stance. If the exercise is done incorrectly, you place a tremendous stress on your lower back.

Thrust Palm in Bow Stance

Riding Goals: Position/Seat, Body Control, Relaxation

This form helps you develop the ability to give aids using your seat and legs while maintaining your upper body's balance. Proficiency in this form will help you keep your horse's outside shoulder from falling out.

Function

Thrust Palm in Bow Stance helps you develop enhanced mobility in your pelvis. It trains your upper body to move independently of your lower body. You gain a new understanding of body alignment and balance, and you unblock the six meridians in your legs and the six in your arms.

Intent

Imagine that you are suspended by a thread from the crown of your head. Imagine that your legs and feet are stone and cannot move. Focus on stretching your fingers beyond your body. Do not lean forward from the hips as you stretch.

Imagine that a pole runs through your body, from the base of your skull down through your torso and pelvis, and then into the ground. When you turn your pelvis, you turn the pole.

Step-by-Step

1 Begin in *Standing Meditation.*

2 Move your feet apart to a double shoulder-width stance with your feet parallel. Place your hands on your hips.

3 Hold your head straight, with your eyes forward. Relax your abdominals and gluteus muscles.

4 Pivot your right foot, on the heel, 90 degrees to the right. This will create a right angle between your two feet.

5 Bend your right leg forward, bringing your right knee over the toes of your right foot while you straighten your left leg.

Steps 2 and 3   *Step 6*   *Step 7*

6 Turn your pelvis, waist, shoulders, and head to the right, so that your torso now faces in the same direction that your right toes are pointing toward.

Initiate the turn from your pelvis. Your goal is to rotate the entire torso as a unit, not simply twist at the waist.

Keep your back straight and vertical. Do not lean forward.

Your left leg is straight, and both feet are flat on the ground.

7 Push your left hand forward, reaching in the direction that your right toes are pointing. As your left hand moves forward from your waist, form a Laing Gong palm, while your right hand, which remains at your right hip, forms a Laing Gong fist (see p. 70). Stretch your left arm and palm as far forward as possible by turning your waist; this will pull your pelvis around a little more and rotate the head of your femur in your hip joint. Hold this stretch for one second or less.

Keep your right knee directly over your toes, your left knee locked, and your left leg straight. The relative position of your knees and feet does not change during the stretch.

As your pelvis turns, the femur of your straight leg rotates slightly. Let your leg rotate as one unit, from your hip all the way down to the ankle of your back foot. This foot should remain flat on the ground throughout the movement. Doing so develops your ability to keep your feet actively quiet while riding.

As you keep your right knee over your toes, feel your weight traveling down into the ground through the ball of your foot.

8 Return to the beginning position and repeat to the left.

There is no mounted version of this exercise. When you are sitting in the saddle, the saddle and the horse prevent you from turning your pelvis completely, limiting the root motion of the form.

The ability to move your pelvis and femur independently of one another is essential to good riding, as it enables you to give aids without losing your connection with your horse. The mobility you gain from this exercise will enable you to give aids with your seat while keeping your legs quiet, and aids with your legs without disturbing your seat.

Ah-Ha!

You will feel a stretch in the hip and thigh of the leg that you hold straight, also across your middle and lower back. When you hold your back in the proper position, you will feel your body spring back to the pre-stretch position.

Ability Transition

As you gain experience with this form, you will notice that the origin of the motion is your pelvis and that everything moves from there. You will feel the stretch in different parts of your body. In the beginning, you may feel most of the stretch in the hips. With time, you'll feel it in your rib cage and the underlying muscles of your abdomen.

Reminder

Remember to keep three things straight in this form: your back, your arm, and your outstretched leg. Be sure to keep the knee of your forward leg over your toes during the stretch. It's common while focusing on the opposing arm and hand to let the knee pull back as you push your hand out, but this backing motion will take away from the stretch in the hips. Also, do not lean forward from the waist while stretching. And, as always, this exercise is designed to align your bones in such a way that they take the force of gravity through your body into the ground. Therefore, being in the correct position prior to the stretch is of paramount importance.

Hold Knee to Chest

Riding Goals: Balance, Awareness, Position/Seat

Hold Knee to Chest teaches you a more effective way to transfer weight from one side of your seat to the other without creating tightness in your seat.

Function

You'll develop enhanced mobility in your lower lumbar vertebrae, abdomen, pelvis, legs, and knees. You will strengthen your legs and improve your balance, while learning how to breathe from the abdomen regardless of body position. The exercise increases your focus and concentration while you are in motion.

Intent

Use your mind to focus *beyond* your body, which, paradoxically, helps you develop a heightened awareness of your actual body position. The root of heaviness is lightness. Before you begin this exercise, imagine that the leg you will lift and your upper body are light as a feather—and the leg you will stand on goes deep into the ground and is as heavy as if it were made of stone.

Step-by-Step

1 Begin in *Standing Meditation.* Place your hands on your hips.

2 Inhale and slowly begin to shift your weight into your left foot as you step forward onto the heel of your right foot. Simultaneously lift your arms straight out in front of you and swing them up until they are directly over your head. Hold your elbows locked. Keep your palms faced in and your fingers pointed up.

3 Stretch your fingers to the sky by bringing your shoulders to your ears.

4 Continue to move your weight forward until 95 percent of your weight is balanced on your right foot. Keep the ball and toes of your left foot on the ground and lift up the heel of the left.

This movement is done while inhaling and should be smooth and fluid throughout.

Step 1

Steps 2, 3, and 4

James On Your Shoulder

Stand straight and light. Imagine that you are being held from above by a thread attached to the top of your head.

5 Without moving forward, allow the last 5 percent of your weight to sink down into your right leg and foot, as if it were sinking through your body and into the ground. Exhale, and at the same time slowly lift your left leg up in front of your body with your knee bent and your toes relaxed and pointing down.

Remember, do not hold your breath. You should be exhaling before you begin to move your body and shift your weight.

6 Circle your arms out and down from over your head, bringing your hands together around your raised knee. Lift the raised knee to your chest.

7 Pull your left knee tight to your body as you let the last bit of breath leave your lungs. Don't force it. Let the stretch help you exhale.

Steps 5 and 6

8 Slowly release your knee and let your left leg stretch down and back to its original position. Allow your toes to touch the ground first, then the ball of your foot with the heel still off the ground. (You will feel a stretch in the foot.) As your left foot touches down, swing your arms back up over your head, palms facing in and fingers stretched to the sky. Allow your whole body to stretch, from toes to fingertips.

9 Continue to shift your weight back into your left foot as your heel comes down. When 100 percent of your weight has shifted into your left foot, step back with the right foot, putting yourself back into a shoulder-width parallel stance. At the same time, drop your arms straight down in front of you until they have returned to their original position.

10 Repeat for the opposite side, this time stepping forward with the left foot and raising your right knee to your chest.

11 Once to the right and once to the left form one complete repetition. Do at least 4 repetitions.

NOTE: This is another exercise for which there is no safe or practical *mounted* version. You will, however, take your new balance and flexibility with you when you ride.

Ah-Ha!

You should eventually feel that your whole body is relaxed during the exercise, and that all your limb movements start and stop at the same time. You will also breathe smoothly and continuously throughout.

Ability Transition

Drop your breath deep into your abdomen before you take the step forward. Exhale slowly as you shift your weight. In the beginning you may lose your balance, wobble, and have to put your leg down to keep from falling. This is natural. Remember that to find and develop your balance, you must first define your imbalance. Only then do you have a scale with which to measure your improvement.

Focus your intent up through your hands as they are stretching to the sky. As you practice and develop your skills, you will notice that you move your upper body very little to shift a great deal of weight. Less and less of your motion will be visible and external; more and more of it will be invisible and internal.

Hold Knee to Chest exercise develops your ability to control your weight and balance as you move both forward and backward as well as to the side. You do this sort of balancing on a micro-muscular scale, and these skills are invaluable for producing transitions, flying-lead changes, and especially big, energetic trots and canters. When done with the proper dedication and effort, this exercise produces tremendous results.

Reminder

Remember, your horse must compensate for your lack of balance when he's supporting you. Any wobble or slight imbalance of yours is felt many-fold by your sensitive horse.

Bend with an Arch

Riding Goals: Position/Seat, Balance, Influencing the Horse

Bend with an Arch helps you gain enhanced mobility in your spine. Your spine is a key element in enabling you to stay balanced over your horse, which then allows the horse to move more freely within his own body.

Function

The exercise enhances your understanding of body alignment and balance. It trains you to keep your spine straight and extended while moving it as one unit. At the same time, it also develops your ability to move your arms, shoulders, and legs independently of your spine. This enhances your ability to remain balanced while you give aids, thereby directing your horse without interfering with him. As with most of these exercises, when done correctly you will feel a very strong sensation of energy rushing through your body as you reach the final position.

Intent

Try visualizing your body as two steel poles stacked end on end. The bottom pole includes your legs; the upper pole includes your torso and head. The poles are hinged at your waist. As you bend, the two poles remain perfectly straight. Only the hinge (your waist) moves.

When you raise your arms, imagine that they are being pulled by your fingertips out and away from your body. Move your awareness from your spine out through your arms into your fingertips.

Step-by-Step

Unmounted

1 Begin in *Standing Meditation*.

2 Lay one hand over the back of your other hand with your fingertips pointed straight down. Tip your head down and look at the backs of your hands.

Step 2

Step 3: Two views

Step 4: Two views

Step 5

Step 6

Step 7

Step 8

3 Lift your arms up, swinging them forward and up directly over your head. Stretch your arms up to the sky by bringing your shoulders to your ears, while keeping your elbows locked.

4 Lower your straightened arms to the sides until your hands, palms up, are at shoulder level. Your back should be arched as much as possible and should remain so throughout the form. Again, stretch your fingers out away from your spine as if someone were gently pulling them.

5 Bend forward from the waist as far as you can without losing any of the arch in your back. As you bend forward, allow your bottom to push back slightly, and let your arms, which remain straight, rotate so that your palms face the ground when you finish the bending motion. Remember that all motion begins from the center; that is, you start the bend by moving your hips back.

6 Drop your arms down toward the ground, crossing your palms. Check that your back is still well arched.

7 Without lifting your body, raise your arms up until they stretch out in front of your head.

8 While maintaining this arms-forward position, lift your torso up, keeping the arch in your back. Raise your body up until you are standing tall, with your arms over your head and your hands stretching to the sky, as in Step 3.

9 Relax your arms and allow them to drop down to your sides, with your palms touching your thighs.

10 Do 3 repetitions.

Mounted

There is no safe way to do this entire exercise mounted, but you can take portions of it into the saddle. The positions in Steps 3 and 4 are great to practice while mounted. They will help you connect your whole body in alignment.

Ah-Ha!

When *Bend with an Arch* is done correctly, you should feel no stress in your back while bending or lifting your body. However, you will feel a tremendous stretch in the backs of your legs and in your gluteus muscles. When you lift your body, use all the muscles in the back of your legs to bring your torso up. At the end of the exercise, while you are dropping your arms, you will feel an overwhelming rush of energy throughout your entire body. This is an excellent opportunity to feel the energy we all possess.

Ability Transition

With practice, the flexibility of your legs and spine will increase and you will develop a greater awareness of your posture, alignment, and balance. After I finish this form, I move with much less tension and have a clearer state of mind.

Reminder

The most important thing to remember in this exercise is to keep your back arched throughout. To arch the back completely you must engage all the smaller muscles that support the individual vertebrae. Any break in the arch becomes the weak link in your structure, and injury may occur. With this in mind, bend only as far as you can without surrendering your arch. This sounds simple, but you would be surprised to know how many people are unaware of when they let go of the arch. Please listen closely to your spine!

Lift a Single Iron Arm

Riding Goals: Balance, Position/Seat

Lift a Single Iron Arm helps you control the left and right vertical balance of your body, ensuring even weight aids in the saddle. When you sit, is your weight even in the saddle? Or, are you heavier on one side than the other? Most of us are one-sided, and this imbalance has a negative effect on the horse's performance.

Function

This exercise engages all the muscles on one side of your spine while allowing the muscles of the opposite side to remain relaxed. Rarely in your daily life do you use one side of the spinal muscles independently of the other side. The exercise's motions make us aware of what would otherwise be an unconscious imbalance. *Lift a Single Iron Arm* works to eliminate one-sidedness by retraining your body to move in harmony between the left and right sides of the spine.

Intent

Hold the arm you lift as straight as an iron rod. There should be no bend whatsoever in your arm from shoulder to fingertips as it is being raised over your head. When pushing your palm toward the sky, feel the stretch from the heel of your foot all the way up through your body to your palm. It should feel as if someone is pulling up on your palm from above, and let that entire side of your body yield to the force. In your mind, completely detach the left side of your body from the right. While you push up one side and feel its lightness, let the other side relax and feel its heaviness.

Step-by-Step

Unmounted

1 Begin in *Standing Meditation*.

2 Slowly lift your left arm straight out to your side with the palm facing down. Your right arm slowly bends at the elbow as you place the back of your right hand against the small of your back.

Step 1

Step 2

Steps 3 and 4

3 Continue to raise your left arm until your hand is directly over your head with your fingers pointing straight up. With your head and eyes, follow the movement of your hand from shoulder level to the stretch position over your head.

Be sure not to let the shoulder of this arm rise with tension. Keep your head and neck straight and the shoulder soft and relaxed.

4 Slowly bring this shoulder toward your ear. Keep your back hand relaxed and the same shoulder down. In other words, don't let the push and stretch of one side create tension in the other.

5 In your raised arm, turn your palm up, so your hand and wrist form a right angle.

6 Point your fingers back at a 45-degree angle, while keeping your hand and wrist in the position in Step 5.

7 Push your palm toward the sky, stretching it upward.

8 Relax your left arm and slowly bring the arm back down, following the same path it took going up, and place it at the small of your back.

9 As your left hand drops below your shoulder, straighten your right arm, swinging your right hand from the small of your back down to your side. The left hand swings in to the small of your back just after the right hand has swung out.

Steps 5, 6, and 7

10 Now your right arm becomes the "iron arm" and swings up, repeating the palm push on the right side. Repeat Steps 2 through 10.

11 Once with the left and once with the right form one complete repetition. Do at least 4 repetitions.

Mounted

Practice *Lift a Single Iron Arm* while riding at the walk on a loose rein or longe line. Ask a friend for assistance.

1 Begin with *Sitting Meditation.*

2 After feeling the connection with your horse, follow the same steps outlined in the unmounted version.

Performing Lift a Single Iron Arm while mounted

Step 5 for both right and left arms: Two views

Ah-Ha!

With practice you will begin to feel the muscles on the relaxed side of your spine letting go before you begin to push your raised palm upward. You will also feel the stretch taking place farther and farther down your spine. Eventually you will feel, in the *unmounted* version, the stretch along the full length of your body, from heel to palm.

Ability Transition

As you develop increasingly enhanced mobility, you may move the hand behind you higher up your back. This more elevated position will relax the shoulder and open the front of the shoulder joint for improved circulation and sensitivity.

Reminder

While pushing the palm up, bring your shoulder to your ear, not the ear to the shoulder. Your spine should be held perfectly straight during the entire exercise. Tilting your head to one side not only takes away from the healing nature of this form, but it also creates or reinforces poor structural alignment.

Summary

In this chapter we have explored a profound territory, a place where you have learned to improve your health and develop your athleticism using Laing Gong. Every time you use these healing exercises, you develop more enhanced mobility in many joints crucial to riding. If you have encountered any difficulties, such as stiffness or pain, I hope you have now clearly identified the root problems and the exercises that can help you heal yourself and overcome these challenges.

You have learned how to move differently—from your quiet center in relaxation rather than through force—and you have become more physically self-aware, so that you can continue to recognize any future "errors" such as tightness, straining, and imbalance. These errors are simply bad habits, or patterns, which you can now identify. When you encounter them, stop, relax, and breathe. Congratulate yourself for noticing the problem, and begin again, watching for the point at which you begin to enter the old pattern. Use your intent and breath to escape that pattern and develop a new pattern, one founded in enhanced mobility. New patterns and lasting change do not come overnight, so you will need to use these exercises with diligence over an extended period of time. Remember what my teacher told me: "There is always a deeper level of relaxation and connection with your body."

Take heart as you work, and know that you have begun to transform your world forever. As one of my mentors regularly reminds me, "We have the power to change the world at anytime by simply changing our perception."

What's Next

In chapter 7, "Application: Bringing It All Together in the Saddle," your focus will shift to riding. You'll work on the quality of the gaits, transitions, bending, lateral work, jumping, and more. Your goal will be to apply to your riding the enhanced mobility you've been developing in this chapter, as well as the enhanced awareness you've developed in the earlier chapters.

Application

7

Bringing It All Together in the Saddle

NOW YOU CAN APPLY THE MIND, BREATH, and body skills you've been learning to riding situations. In this chapter, you'll encounter questions to expand your awareness. I ask you to remember experiences from previous chapters, and I explain and show you how they can be used now as tools to enhance your riding.

Ride from Your Center

As you continue to practice the exercises in this book, I can promise that you'll experience the following:

• Your body will increasingly act as one cohesive unit with all your aids coming from your center. Taking advantage of your innate strengths and working with the laws of nature (gravity, momentum, and centripetal force), you'll make your horse responsive to the slightest changes in your body.

• You will experience a connection like never before with your horse. You will know that your horse is your greatest teacher, and that *he* has picked *you* as a student.

• With clear intent you will project transitions out in front of you and your horse. From a foundation of smooth, rhythmic breathing, your timing will be flawless; transitions will appear as if there was a silent agreement made by you and your horse to change at a predetermined spot.

These are my promises. I do not take them lightly. I have seen them come true for hundreds of riders.

This is simple, but not easy. The letting go of old ideas and habits is a challenge— mentally, physically, and even emotionally. You may experience joy and fear, laughter and tears. All of these are common, and healthy. In all of this, remember that words will get you no closer to your truth. You will need to practice on and off your horse.

Ride from your center. Abdominal breathing changes the volume of your center, making it bigger, and therefore easier for you to stay balanced. Remember your breath is the vehicle that takes your mind into your body and to your center. Therefore, always know where your breath is. Without it, nothing can change—and with it, nothing is impossible. Your horse can feel a fly on his rump, and he can feel when you hold your breath.

Having a Conversation with Your Horse

When you're in the saddle you need to have a give and take with your horse. It's a conversation, not a lecture. Conversations require that you listen as well as speak, and you can't listen if you're always speaking. This is the basis of a respectful relationship. Some of us do prefer to lecture and lead, but you can't do this all the time. And I

The Most Helpful Question

What is my most fundamental and helpful question for you?

"Where is your breath?"

Search your body with a quiet, calm mind. Maybe you'll find it up high in your chest; maybe it'll be down deep in your belly. In either case, your mind will be focused inward. You'll be connected in mind and body. With a heightened awareness and sensitivity developed by the exercises in previous chapters, you'll move your body with enhanced mobility.

But don't always wait for me to ask you this question. Make it your own! At any time—while exercising or riding, or while just going to the post office or market—you will always benefit from asking yourself this most helpful question: "Where is my breath?"

would suggest that what you get in these situations is compliance, but is that all you want from your horse? If so, you're missing a profound opportunity.

As you've come so far in this book, which sees the horse as our greatest teacher, I will assume that you are interested in having a conversation with your horse. In fact, you do this any time that you join centers with him.

Let's also be clear about what I am *not* suggesting: passivity. When you ride, you *actively* direct your horse. You are responsible for both the horse and yourself. You are leading, but you're not *only* leading.

Practically speaking, any time you attempt to join centers with a force greater than yourself you can't just lead—you're not in a position of power and you will be overwhelmed. (Remember the first three Principles of Tai Chi: *Use the mind, not force*; *Never oppose force with force*; and, *Yield and overcome*.)

Given that you must direct your horse—having him walk, trot, canter, jump—how do you do this while maintaining a conversation with your horse? You *follow, match, and lead*.

Strength as Weakness

Your strengths can trap you and limit your progress. It is human nature to want to "put your best foot forward." It's easy to rely on your strengths, but it takes courage to look at and develop your weaknesses.

For example, if you have a beautiful trot but it takes you a few strides after the transition to "settle in" to this trot, then the transition represents your greatest opportunity for improvement. Practicing transitions will be hard. It will demand dropping out of what is comfortable (the trot), only to return to the uncomfortable over and over again.

With thoughtful consideration of the Tai Chi principles and your newly acquired sensitivity of mind and body, you're ready to take on this challenge. If you persevere and continue the work you've begun in this book, I am confident that you will make the leap to the next level in your riding.

Follow—Match—Lead

Perhaps the quickest way to explain *follow—match—lead* is by example. While this approach applies to all riding situations, here's how it works when you ride a posting trot:

1 You *follow* when the rising energy from the horse's hind legs lifts you out of the saddle;

2 you *match* when you reach the height of your posting; and

3 you *lead* when you sit and apply your driving aid.

Follow—match—lead can be applied to any energy that moves in rhythm, in waves or circles of force. The concept itself is a continuous cycle, constant and yet ever-changing. You are always in one of these three states, and you always move through them in this order.

Sometimes this concept is difficult to feel while riding, and this is often because the speed at which the cycle is revolving is too fast; we don't have enough time to feel the phases and react. This is one of the reasons we usually learn a new movement at a slow speed. As children, we walk before we run. As riders, we walk before we trot. If when you are riding you can't feel the energy cycles, relax and don't worry. With practice you will learn how to follow, match, and lead at this gait, too. At these moments it is enough to "know" in your mind that you are still part of this flow of energy—most likely just following. And surprisingly enough, knowing that you can not always lead often has a calming effect on the mind.

Let's look at this cycle in more detail:

Follow

The horse moves, and you allow him to influence you at that moment. He sets the rhythm, and your body follows him. You follow him, relaxed and listening. You may follow his motion for a half-second, or for ten seconds. Once you've relaxed and followed, you're ready to match.

Match

Now you are connected with the horse's motion, and your mind, breath, and body match him. You're not ahead of or behind the motion, but synchronized and neutral. You are relaxed in your body. Your mind is calm and aware. You are ready to lead.

Lead

You are the directing partner, and you lead your horse by indicating direction, speed, and impulsion. You communicate with your aids within his rhythm. Now that you've communicated your intent, you follow the greater force of the horse.

Returning to our earlier analogy to a conversation:

- when your horse is speaking, you are listening (*following*);
- then there is a moment of quiet (*matching*); and finally,
- when you are speaking (*leading*), your horse is listening.

The conversation flows on and on.

Practically, you already know that aids are most effective when they are precise and brief. After giving the aid, you then need to listen (by following and then matching) in order to assess your horse's response. If the horse did not respond as you wished, you give another aid—lead again. (Of course, this assumes that you are giving the correct aids at the right time.) As you and your horse improve, you'll spend more and more of your time matching, and less and less of your time following or leading. The next time you ride, think about identifying which state you're in, and when you move into another state.

How do you learn to follow, match, and lead? Just as the rhythm of your breath is the key to timing in your body, so is breath the key to maintaining the connection between you and your horse. All the work you have done so far in this book has prepared you to be with your horse in this way.

Let's look at another example of *follow—match—lead*: jumping.

You lead in the approach, match, in the takeoff, and follow over the fence. Now, decompose that sequence into a more detailed, second-by-second series of states:

- When you're approaching the jump, you're leading, and you're directing the horse's attention to the fence.

- Then you follow and match, sensing his response—if he's focused, you can stay matched. If you sense him starting to consider an evasion, you lead again, then follow and match as you assess his response.

  If you need to adjust your striding, you lead, and then return to following and matching.

- As soon as he takes off, he leads, and you follow and then match him in the air and through the landing.

Remember that if you are leading, your horse is following. If you are following, your horse is leading.

Now, consider your own riding. Whether over fences or on the flat, ask yourself these questions:

- Am I always trying to lead?

- Do I follow too often, and let my horse lead me?

Tai Chi's Connection with Follow—Match—Lead

In the discussion of *follow—match—lead*, you may have noticed its underlying complementary nature: it involves, like Yin and Yang, a circular, flowing exchange. You never oppose the force of the horse. Through follow, match, and lead, you redirect the force of the horse from your center.

Expand your awareness, become enlightened, and anything is possible. Otherwise, you will remain trapped in your old ways of thinking and moving. If you continue to do the work you've been learning in this book, you will become enlightened, and you will learn more deeply and quickly.

Does "enlightenment" sound too grandiose or unattainable? Here's another saying from the *Tao Te Ching*: "Knowing others is wisdom. Knowing yourself is enlightenment."

When I first went to Wen Mei Yu, my first Tai Chi teacher, and asked to study with her, she turned me down, saying, "You have too many bad habits. In fact, you have the best bad habits I've ever seen." I came to understand how they permeated my whole body. I had practiced for years noticing only the outside of my body, never looking deeper and never addressing my weaknesses.

Can any rider gain enlightenment? Yes, it's possible, even necessary, because your bad habits don't go away on the horse. You, like all of us, need to retrain yourself to use your body well. You will need to free yourself from fear and let go of old habits. You will have to overcome barriers of mind, desire, willingness, and intent. You will have to be vigilant because as soon as your awareness fades, your unconscious habits will drift back in to fill the space. Enlightenment, and better riding, are won through many, many small efforts, day after day. As Lao Tzu wrote: "A good traveler has no fixed plans, and is not intent on arriving."

Probably the good riders you admire are wise. And the best riders are enlightened. They've earned that knowledge through years of practice. You, too, can know the wisdom of riding a horse and become enlightened by knowing your own body.

Developing Your Program

The exercises in the previous chapters are excellent riding warm-ups. Do the ground versions of these forms before you ride. Once you've learned them, all these exercises take less than twenty minutes. Pick your four favorites, or perhaps your four least favorites (to develop your weaknesses), and do them before you saddle your horse. Once you're on your horse, repeat the *mounted* versions.

Just before you mount up, ask yourself these questions:

- Do I release my stress and tension before I ride?
- Am I communicating unnecessary tension and stress to my horse?
- Do I remember that my horse also needs to shift into his work?
- Do I always warm him up and cool him down?

It's nearly impossible to keep the mind–body connection continuous and unbroken. And it's also difficult to keep the stresses and fears of the world and society out of your mind and body. You can, however, reduce these tension-creating distractions within a few minutes by using these exercises as warm-ups prior to riding. You and your horse will be happier and more productive.

Intent

In the coming sections I'll focus on the trot, canter, transitions, bending, and lateral work. Before you start, ask yourself, "Who knows how to canter better—my horse or I? Who was born knowing how to canter?" I ask these questions because all too often I see riders whose horse is not moving well, and so they think that they should teach their horse how to move. This may, in fact, be true. But before we assume it is, let's also make explicit what this assumes. It assumes that your horse is sound, that your saddle and bit fit well, that you ride balanced, centered, and connected with your horse, and that you have sufficient knowledge to teach him. If you're unsure of how you'd assess any of these, seek professional help from your veterinarian, chiropractor, farrier, saddle-fitter, riding instructor, or horse trainer. Let's assume that you've passed all these tests with flying colors, and now return to you, your horse, and using intent.

Using *follow—match—lead*, you will ask (lead) and then follow. To guide your horse in these movements, you

- must be clear in your intent before you commit to an aid, and
- must move your body from its center with your mind.

Your intent leads your horse.

First, feel where you're going. Put your mind there and then let the body follow. In the *Side Step* exercise (p. 43), you practiced engaging your intent, and letting your body follow. You "melted" the muscles in front of your body. You didn't move until 100 percent of your weight was shifted.

Practice this same pattern in your mounted work. Without clear intent you will move awkwardly, without good timing, and without full body unity. Your horse will never quite know what you are asking for, and in your frustration you will very likely "over aid" and use force. Force always creates a separation between you and your horse. Often your horse will actively avoid your forced direction in an attempt to relieve the discomfort you're causing.

Intent and Jumping

You can project your intent out in front of you at any given moment. With a little experience and practice, you can even place your intent in two places at one time. In fact, there are no limits to where and how you project your intent. For example, in a jumping round, you may in the same moment be completely aware of the state of your body while projecting your intent out beyond an upcoming jump. It is the same as putting your mind into the balls of your feet prior to letting your weight move forward (see *Standing Meditation*, p. 37).

You've probably heard the saying, "Throw your heart over the fence, and your horse will follow." With your focus out beyond the jump, your awareness is heightened and your horse is reassured about where the two of you are headed. Your expanded awareness makes your sensitivity acute, and therefore you experience no need to micromanage your position and your horse. Remember it's your horse that is going to jump the fence, not you.

The exercises coming up in this chapter follow a slightly different format from those in earlier chapters. You'll find an "Opening the Gates" section that will connect each exercise back to your earlier work on the Eight Gates.

Aids from Your Center

"The center is the source of all sense and perception"

(*Tai Chi Classics*)

Only when your center is loosened can you move with agility and coordination. It is as if your center is the hub of a wheel that's constantly rotating. All motion begins at the center.

With a loosened center, you can "talk" to your horse using a whisper instead of a loud voice. Most of us never learned how to move from the center. Instead of using the core muscles in the body to move your center, we tend to use the bigger, dominant muscles of our limbs and torso to pull our center this way and that.

Here's a little test.

1 If you're not sitting, sit.

2 Move your left seat bone forward in your chair.

How easy was it? Did you have to think about how to do it? Did you pull your seat forward with your left thigh, or did you push with your gluteus muscles? Did your weight shift to the left? Did you clench or brace any muscles? Did you hold your breath as you attempted to move your seat?

All of the above results are symptoms—symptoms that disconnect you from your horse. If you were riding, how much connection with the horse would you have given up to simply move your seat bone forward?

1   Try it again. Only this time I would like you to become aware of your belly
    button, which is a useful landmark for locating our center.

2   Now move your belly button to the right by turning your waist to the right.
    Feel your left seat bone move forward as your center—belly button—moves
to the right. Notice the ease in which you move your seat bones when shift your
focus to moving your center.

You may be accustomed to shifting your weight by leaning, and by pushing and
pulling from outside your center. The approach throughout this book, however, is
to move from inside our center. When we move in this way we move with less
effort and more fluidity and speed. Moving your belly button can become a highly
effective focal point for directing your primary aids while staying connected with
your horse.

The belly button idea is one of many techniques you'll learn in this chapter to help
you stay centered and free of tension while riding. Your aids will effortlessly redirect your horse when they are directed from your center. When you join centers
with your horse, "your" center includes the horse's. You can redirect the horse by
simply moving your own center because you and your horse share a joined center.

In classical Tai Chi, students are challenged to discover how to redirect the force of
1000 pounds using only 4 ounces of force. While you're probably tempted to think
that this feat is almost impossible, you need to realize that you are already well on
your way to possessing these skills.

Refining the Walk

At the walk you can develop your skills of awareness, breathing, and intent. Because the walk is the slowest gait, you have time to go through the checklist of mind, breath, and body. You can identify and address the root cause of what you do in the saddle. In addition, you'll learn how to energize your horse's walk.

Before You Mount

Revisit the *Horse Stance* (p. 56). Push your knees out and feel the tendons under your seat bones tighten. Now arch your lower back and feel the tendons soften. Realize that you are in a very weak position, one that you want to avoid. Breathe deeply and slowly and soften your lower back. Fix this by redirecting your breath toward the lower back so you expand and open the Ming Meng.

Step-by-Step

1 When you mount, begin in *Sitting Meditation* (p. 40). Where is your breath? If it's not already in your Dain Tian, direct it with your mind down into your Dain Tian. Search for tension in your body and ask yourself why it is there. Let tension drop through your bones, down through the horse, and into the ground.

2 When you are completely relaxed and aware, then signal your horse to walk. As your horse moves forward underneath you, listen to your body. Again, are you arching your back in an effort to "sit up straight"? If you are, you now know that you are adversely affecting your structural alignment. You are blocking the energy of the horse at your waist and putting weight on the horse's forehand through the leverage created by your stiff spine.

3 Instead of sitting up straight, fill your belly with your breath. This "filling" acts to support a straight and sensitive spine without restricting your ability to move with your horse. You're opening Gate 1: The Dain Tian.

4 After you feel your abdomen relax and expand, move your attention to your lower back and allow your breath to fill and soften it. You're opening Gate 2: The Ming Meng.

5 Feel how your horse moves underneath you; feel the power of his movement and how your body moves with the force.

Your horse is always moving you, because he's bigger and stronger. Keep your head and eyes up—don't look down at the horse.

Now is the time to connect with your horse, not to direct him. You can connect with his rhythmic motion. Instructors of therapeutic riding rely on that motion to help their riders. The horse's rhythm is your ally. All riding is therapeutic: the horse's action is like a massage that helps you move your body and regain natural mobility.

Maintain your structural integrity. Let the rhythm of your horse teach you how to move. Join with that rhythm. At this point, your goal should be to let go, not "to do something." Excess body motion affects the horse's stride—for instance, making him tense and quick in his front legs. Relax. Let yourself be moved. Breathe. Follow.

Ask a friend to watch your upper body movement. Are you "pushing" toward the pommel of the saddle, with too much forward movement, and not the same motion in the back?

Move your awareness to your center; see if you can find the left-right rise and fall of the horse's hindlegs. This vertical motion combined with the constant forward motion of you and your horse acts to create a figure-eight shaped motion in your center (see drawing).

Think of your pelvis moving inside a sphere, which is your center (your expanded center—don't forget that your joining centers with your horse). Rather than focusing on your horse's movement, search inside your center and locate that three-dimensional, figure-eight motion. Your relaxed and following seat allows the energy of the horse to move through you in this pattern. When you have become aware of the motion inside, you are truly connected with your horse. Realize that once again you have used the path of mind, breath, and body to connect with your horse.

James On Your Shoulder

Remember the first and only rule, "Smile."

When you want to know what your horse is doing, feel, don't look. Trust that you can sense everything you need to know about your horse without using your eyes.

A figure-eight motion in your center.

6 Walk a circle, and investigate the cadence of your breath. Are you taking one long breath in, accompanied by one long breath out? Or, do you inhale on a count like, "*in* one, two; *out* one, two"?

Find the relationship between the cadence of your breath and the strides of your horse. How many steps does your horse take while you're inhaling, and how many while you're exhaling? By changing the cadence or rhythm of your breathing you can influence your horse's gait. Slow, deep breaths tell the horse to relax and lengthen his strides, decreasing his tempo. Quicker, more energetic breaths pick up the horse's tempo.

7 Quicken the rhythm of your breath. Don't change the depth of your breathing, but just try to take in the same amount of air a little faster.

For example, instead of inhaling and exhaling on a two-count, inhale on a three-count, and exhale to a four-count. Play with this exercise until you experience how you can refine your horse's walk simply by exercising your breath. Be careful not to use your leg on the horse while practicing this exercise. The goal is to develop your breath as a riding aid. The goal is not a spirited, energized walk, but the quality of the walk that results from using this aid.

CAUTION: Don't hyperventilate. If you begin to feel light-headed, you are trying too hard. Relax and slow your respiration until you feel centered, and then try again taking shorter breaths.

8 As your horse's gait quickens, so does the figure-eight motion in your center. Imagine that the eight is getting bigger and moving a little faster.

Remember that your breath is merely an aid in creating the mind–body connection. Once connected, the motion of your center influences your horse most. The figure eight is a great tool that allows you to focus on your center without tightening up. Practice changing the shape of the eight. How does your center affect the tempo and energy of your horse?

9 See if you can get more motion in your lower back. Can you relax more and expand your lower back so that you can actually feel the force of the horse's hind end move through your Ming Meng toward the front of your body? When this happens, it will feel as if your lumbar vertebrae are stretched open as if suspended from above. This is an extremely effective method for healing a sore back and loosening a tight lower back.

Opening the Gates

At the walk, you are concerned with three gates: The Dain Tian, Ming Meng, and the Back of the Heart. By directing your breath into these areas, you soften and expand your body—opening the gates. The ability to open any of the Eight Gates while riding depends on your practice on the ground. Without sufficient time spent discovering and becoming aware of these areas, your work on the horse will be greatly hampered.

Review these exercises to help open the Dain Tian, Ming Meng, and the Back of the Heart:

- *Abdominal Breathing* (p. 90)
- *Open the Ming Meng* (p. 99)
- *Thrust Palm in Bow Stance* (p. 146)

> *Rider Insight, Cindy:* "When I learned to open the two lower gates, it felt as if I were riding inside my horse. As soon as I let go with the back of my heart, I felt as if I were riding on a big squishy ball instead of a saddle."

Reminder

If you don't feel connected, go back to *Counting Your Breath* (p. 97).

If you feel tight, revisit these exercises to unlock your body:

- *Embracing the Moon* (p. 102)
- *Hold the Sky with Both Hands* (p. 138)
- *Neck Turns* (p. 121)
- *Spread Your Chest* (p. 126)

Because you practiced these exercises on the ground, your body will remember them and the awareness will follow you into the saddle. If you haven't done these on the ground, don't expect them to work magically on the horse. There are no shortcuts.

In a similar way, there are no shortcuts on your horse either. For example, the beginning of a great trot starts with the end of a great walk. In your upward transition, you must end with a great walk to experience a seamless transition upward into the trot. You take these abilities into the trot and canter, where the motion is bigger. You learn them at the walk, because you can't effectively learn them at the faster, more energetic gaits. The bigger the movement, the harder it is to release and let go of the tension that binds the body.

Using Observation to See Energy Moving

The idea of seeing energy might conjure up visions of metaphysical and New Age followers gazing into auras and looking at colors and light. While I believe that some people really do see forms of energy that most of us miss, the energy that I'm describing can be seen by everyone who knows where to look—as I'll explain in a moment.

While most of us cannot explain the mechanics of gravity, we sense it and can anticipate its effects (a suspended ball, for instance, will drop when released). While riders might not be able to explain the mechanics of energy flows between horse and rider, we can sense and anticipate its effects (a connected walk, for instance, will propel our center through a figure-eight pattern).

Because we've lived with gravity since birth, we have developed a deep, largely unconscious sense of its effects. None of us has, in contrast, spent nearly as much time on horseback—for many of us it's a relatively brief encounter perhaps two or three times a week—so it's no wonder that we are less sensitive and skilled at seeing these horse-rider energy flows.

When I look at horse and rider I see them as one organic whole. Your two separate energies combine to make one force greater than the sum of your two parts. The way that I see the movement of energy move from the horse into the rider and back into the horse is first by watching the way the wrinkles of your clothing move as you ride. It's the same way that I can be sitting inside a building and know without any doubt that the wind is blowing outside by observing the undulating movements of a flag. By paying close attention to how the wrinkles move, I can see how the energy of your horse is moving through you.

For example, if I'm watching you at the trot, I might see the wrinkles in the back of your shirt roll horizontally upward from your lower back (Ming Meng), traveling straight up and out the neck of your shirt. This tells me that the energy of your horse is not being redirected back into the whole–you and your horse–but is instead being lost out the top of your head.

See for yourself. Watch the wrinkles in the shirt of a rider who is one with her horse. You will see the wrinkles move up toward the upper back–when they reach Gate 4: The Back of the Heart, the wrinkles dissipate out toward the shoulders, where they disappear. This motion of the wrinkles tells me that the rider's energy has been redirected at Gate 4, forward out Gate 3: The Front of the Heart, and down the arms through the reins back to the horse.

The movement of the wrinkles in the rider's shirt mirrors the internal flow of energy through his body.

Watch the rhythm of the horse in the rider's shirt wrinkles. If the two are connected, there will be a common rhythm between the move-ment of the horse's tail and the rider's clothing. If the rider you are watching wears her hair in a ponytail, look for the movement of the ponytail in relation to the horse's tail and mane.

Root Problems

Usually you are more concerned with the horse than yourself; this outward focus distracts you from your part of the union with your horse. Your body goes into a sort of autopilot, where tension can run rampant. For instance, this tension may lead you to hold your breath. Or, if you are breathing, you might breathe high into a tight chest. In an attempt to get a more energetic walk or to push your horse forward, you may be tempted to use force to contort, push, and pull with your seat. Underlying all these symptoms is a single root problem—not relaxing and breathing deep into your abdomen.

If you find yourself in this tense predicament, don't get caught up by the situation. Take a good, deep belly breath. Relax. Just start again—hit your own "reset" button by returning to the beginning of the exercise. If you still find yourself becoming tense, return to the unmounted exercises. Remember that all the time you spend in the unmounted exercises is an investment—not time lost from riding. Working on the ground gives you an opportunity to focus on your mind, breath, and body without any distractions. These exercises then pay dividends when you ride. Please don't think of the unmounted exercises as something to graduate from.

To improve your riding at the walk, review these two exercises:

- *Hold the Sky with Both Hands*, for moving your spine as a single unit (p. 138)
- *Thrust Palm in Bow Stance*, for creating independent motion of your torso and pelvis (p. 146)

Smooth, Invisible Transitions

Your riding goal should be to think a transition and have your horse respond by executing your thought. This effortless harmony can become real. You've probably seen riding masters who can ride any horse and stay connected with the horse's every action, and all the while they ride without any obvious aids. Keep those images in mind.

The key to seamless transitions is timing. Without it, your transitions are left to chance. I have observed many riders whose walk, trot, and canter are beautiful, but their transitions are disjointed. For example, I often see walk-trot transitions in which the rider asks for a transition and then struggles for two or three strides, until the horse gets the message and picks up the trot. Typically, I see this pattern repeated with nearly every transition, upward or downward.

In these situations, the rider, within the first moments of asking for and not getting the trot, tenses and begins to overuse aids that are ineffective mainly because of their inappropriate timing, nothing else. As the rider pushes, pulls, and adjusts, the only thing that's accomplished is putting her body into an unbalanced position. Now the horse faces two challenges: unclear aids and an unbalanced and unbalancing rider. Remember that when you're giving an aid, you are leading (*follow—match—lead*). *An unbalanced rider cannot lead the horse to anything but an unbalanced state.*

At this point, several things can happen:

- The horse and rider can continue in imbalance, or
- they can recover balance by relaxing back into a walk, or
- the horse can take over the lead, make the transition and establish the trot, and then the rider can follow and match—in essence recovering her balance thanks to the horse.

But this whole struggle is entirely avoidable.

The problem starts before any physical aid is given; it starts in the rider's mind. Most transitions are asked for at a specific point predetermined by the rider or trainer, such as a letter in a dressage arena, a cone in the reining pen, or some other landmark. When the transition point is defined in this way, it is nearly impossible to maintain a rhythmic connection with the horse as you approach "The Spot." Predetermining the exact point or spot of transition creates in the mind an invisible vertical plane in time and space at which the transition must take place. It's much like running up to a stream to jump over it and realizing when you get closer that you are on the wrong lead to jump. You adjust by taking half- or stutter-steps in an attempt to get the right lead. This throws your body out of rhythm and usually results in a weak—and wet—jump.

When you use a specific spot to plan your transitions, this self-imposed starting line often causes you to barge into your transitions regardless of whether or not you and your horse are ready. In this case, the problem lays in your perception, not your ability; that is, you have forced your timing and fouled yourself up.

Step-by-Step

Here's the technique I use to help create seamless and effortless transitions.

1 Assuming that you and your horse are well warmed up, pick a spot in the arena where you would like to have the transition take place.

2 Envision a sphere large enough to contain both you and your horse and see that sphere surrounding the spot where the transition will happen.

Now there is no longer a line, but rather an area in which you perform the transition. It's important to *see* it, not just *think* it. I personally envision a large soap bubble for my sphere, like the ones I blew as a child. I see all the colors of the rainbow swirling inside its shimmering surface.

3 Next, close your eyes and see and feel a perfect trot in your mind's eye. You and your horse move in complete harmony, as if you were trotting on air.

4 Open your eyes and look again at the bubble, and see that perfect trot happening inside the bubble. With your intent you project what you created in your mind forward into the sphere, so now the perfect trot waits for you and your horse to ride into it.

Instead of having to focus on a tense, thin line in space, you can now focus on entering the bubble from a balanced and quiet walk, completely ready to follow your horse into the perfect trot that awaits you. By taking a few moments to change your perception and expand your awareness, you can achieve amazing results in your transitions.

Opening the Gates

You'll use three gates in the process of creating and projecting the trot: Gate 3: The Front of the Heart, Gate 7: The Upper Pass, and Gate 8: The Crown. Open the Upper Pass and Crown to create the trot in your mind's eye. I think of it like a movie projector. Your mind's eye is the film—the image of the trot you envision; the Upper Pass is the lens, focusing this image forward, keeping it clear and real; and the Crown is the light source that projects the image. Now, to carry this metaphor just a bit further, we need to direct that image to a particular place. Your *open heart* and your *intent* direct the created image to the sphere.

Reminder

If you haven't practiced *Walking Backward* (p. 62), you are missing an important experience that is necessary in order to make this technique effective. Remember that the power of this technique comes from expanding your awareness to change your perception.

Your mind, breath, and body must be connected at the walk before you attempt a walk-trot transition. If you have trouble using this technique, return to the unmounted exercises to build your skills and awareness.

Upward Transition: Walk to Trot

You have probably experienced those gratifying moments when your horse flowed from walk to trot, or from trot to walk. The transitions were calm, with one gait rolling into the next with no bouncing or undue effort. You can help yourself have transitions like this all the time by first projecting your intent and then staying focused on your body. Your horse will feel subtle adjustments instead of "loud" aids. You'll relive that moment of perfection, following the path of mind, breath, and body.

Before You Ask

The walk-trot transition can be executed in a moment when your timing is correct. As you project your intent into the coming trot, however, ride the walk you're still in.

On a physical level, a smooth transition starts at the last stride of the gait leading into it. To enjoy a good walk-trot transition, ride that last walk step with the same quality of rhythm and impulsion as the previous steps. Be entirely physically present and aware of every moment in the walk. Savor it! Taste it as you would a fine wine—without rushing, enjoying it for what it is, rather than anticipating the taste of what you're going to eat or drink next.

As you maintain this intense physical connection with the walk, mentally use your intent to envision and project your perfect trot. There is no contradiction here: physically, you're entirely present in the moment; mentally, you're anticipating the coming trot. Remember the exercise *Walking Backward* (p. 62), in which you experienced the power and independence of your physical body and your intent.

Most of the transition problems I see arise because riders *abandon the walk before the transition*. They slip into a no-man's land—neither walk nor trot—and lose their connection with their horse.

Maintain your "bone-to-leather" connection in your seat. Stay with your horse. Inhale when you think of the trot. Exhale when you ask.

Make your aid clear and concise. I see riders whose horses have been aided to dullness, and usually it's because the rider's body gets in the way. Could this be you? Don't let your body get in the way of clear communication.

In giving an aid with your outside leg, did you move your upper body out, up, and away from your leg that applied the aid? Think back to your experience of *Side Step* (p. 43). Did you lean to take the step? If yes, then you're now seeing that same movement habit here in the trot transition. Don't lean with your body to get your outside leg back, otherwise your horse will have to compensate for your shifting weight before he can respond to your aid.

Don't leave your body's position entering the transition to chance. I'll repeat my most fundamental question: "Where is your breath?" When asking for the trot, are you breathing in or out? Experiment and determine whether your horse changes gaits better when you're inhaling or exhaling.

Step-by-Step

1 When you mount, begin in *Sitting Meditation*. Complete your normal warm-up.

2 For the first round, try asking for the transition while inhaling. The very first communication with your horse when asking for the trot should be your breath. Breathe in and expand the space under your rib cage. Expand the Ming Meng. You get an instant connection for the transition. Your body will be ready to receive the change in force in your horse's gait as he picks up the trot.

3 Lead your body with your mind. Use your intent to create the trot you want; project it in front of you. Don't worry about moving your body into that trot— your horse will do that for you. By projecting your intent forward, you have created the new space into which you and your horse will move. Let your body remain quiet, correct, and ready to lead.

Listen to your body, and feel whether or not you tense your seat when you prepare for the change. Do you hold your breath? If so, think about exhaling into the trot.

4 Give your aid. As your horse picks up the trot, you pick up your breath. You have now changed the rhythm and your breathing must follow. Find the new rhythm of

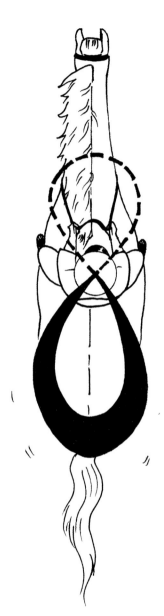

The figure-eight motion in your center at the trot.

your breath. It will be dictated by the bigger motion of the horse in your body.

Revisit the figure-eight pattern you practiced in *Refining the Walk* (p. 176). That figure eight is still there, only now because of the suspension present in the trot it follows a more vertical ellipse with a kind of over-the-top-feeling rather than the flatter, more horizontal plane it follows at the walk (see drawing).

Opening the Gates

Begin the transition by energizing Gate 8: The Crown and Gate 2: The Ming Meng. In the last moments of the walk, pay close attention to the Ming Meng, keeping it open throughout the transition. The power of the horse rising into your body can cause you to tighten your heart. Exhaling into the transition will help you avoid any such tightening and help you maintain your connection into the trot.

Reminder

Remember that your breath is a powerful and versatile tool. You may find that you have better transitions while exhaling rather than inhaling. Whatever the case may be, your fluid, rhythmic breathing is the key to staying connected with the horse through transitions. I recommend that you take the time to discover the treasures hidden in this exercise. Your goal should not be getting the trot, but understanding the transition.

Root Causes

Concentrating on leg and rein aids pulls us out of awareness of our center. Remember that all change comes from our center. Check yourself for over-reliance on these external aids. Are you perhaps using them to help you balance? Breathe and shift your focus to your center as you quiet these aids.

Downward Transition: Trot to Walk to Halt

You've followed the mind, breath, and body path to the upward transition. Now you'll use the same aids to transition down to the walk and then the halt. You may want to refer back to your earlier work in *Breathing to a Halt or Walk* (p. 112).

In transitioning down to a walk from the trot, your center must lead—as it must in any transition. The motion and rhythm of your pelvis must slow without disconnecting from your horse. The most frequent root cause of this disconnection is tensing the muscles around the seat. This tensing is known as holding or bracing.

Bracing changes the movement of your pelvis and can cause you to bounce to a walk—not what we want. The aid I often see in this transition is the rider holding her breath as she tightens her abdominal muscles to slow the pelvis. This tightening or squeezing with the abs and bracing in the lower back (Ming Meng) does slow the pelvis, by restricting the movement of the lower lumbar. If you do this, you cut yourself in half energetically, and you cannot redirect the horse's energy down to the walk.

Instead, use your breath to slow your pelvis without tightening the lower back. Breathe down deep into your belly and as your diaphragm pushes down, your visceral cavity expands, changing its volume with the pressure. This change in pressure slows your pelvis without restricting its motion through holding with the external muscles of your abdomen. You need those external muscles to be soft and sensitive to negotiate the changing rhythm in your body as your horse slows to the walk. Holding your breath negates your aid and disconnects you from your horse.

Before You Ask

Slowing your horse with your body alone is ineffective. First, think about the transition: clarify your intent, and let your body go where your mind has already gone.

Expand your awareness outward. Think of the exercise *Walking Backward* (p. 62), in which you experienced your environment moving independently. Use this experience to see your riding environment slowing down and coming to a walk.

Imagine your Ming Meng gate closing slightly. This will slow the movement in your lower back and open your Dain Tian. In this state the weight of your body will fall slightly forward in your seat and slow your pelvis.

James On Your Shoulder

Don't get frustrated if you can't breathe into the walk from the trot on your first try. Feel your breath sink into your abdomen and imagine it sinking down through your body into your horse. Awareness is the start.

Opening the heart gates at the trot prior to getting the walk can be a challenge. It requires letting go of fear. Fear in all its forms closes the heart; in fact, it slams it closed. Most of us have built up armor in the form of a closed heart. We have done so to protect ourselves and now it keeps us separated from our horse. Deep healing and connection can take place when we let go of our old fears.

Step-by-Step

1 Put your mind into your center. As you trot, feel the motion of your center and connect with it before you slow it. Use your mind's eye to see your pelvic bone: see its rocking in relationship to the rhythm of your breath.

2 When your mind and body are connected through your breath, your horse will walk when you ask. Ask as you exhale, letting this be your first aid. During the down transition your motion may be slightly ahead of your horse. You need, therefore, to redirect your energy down into your horse through the Dain Tian. If you don't, you'll be pushed forward out of your seat, and your weight will fall onto the horse's forehand.

In addition, you can compensate for the transition by keeping the Back of the Heart gate open throughout. I think of it like an open parachute slowing down my upper body. This opening helps to redirect the momentum down through your spine into your seat, rather than forward through the Front of the Heart gate, again pushing you forward.

Ideally, you'll have both your heart gates open, and this will help your upper body to be balanced, and your hands quiet and sensitive. All of this allows your seat to remain soft and deep and keeps you from bouncing forcefully down on the horse's back. Opening the front heart gate also helps open the Chi Who gates, and their opening enhances the strength and sensitivity of the hands and arms.

Opening the Gates

Closing the Ming Meng slightly while keeping the Back of the Heart and Dain Tian wide open will help your down transitions. Keeping the Back of the Heart open helps you avoid tightening and getting pushed forward in the saddle. This tightening often originates in using the reins to slow the horse.

If you're having trouble keeping the front heart gate open, try this: reach up with one arm and place your hand on top of your head; keep your elbow pointing out to the side. This position opens the Chi Who gate (below your collarbone), and this, in turn, helps open the front heart gate. Now gently lower your arm and retake the reins, paying close attention all the while to maintain the softness in the Chi Who. If you have a tendency to brace in your chest and shoulders, you will feel the tension return to the heart and Chi Who as soon as the arm drops. It's simply a bad habit, and you now have the tools to change it.

Reminder

Remember the more your pelvis moves, the less your upper body moves. Your lower lumbar moves and dissipates the motion of your upper body. If you brace in the chest, everything else moves. Holding on with your seat, you fight physics. Surrender your center and spine to the rhythm of the horse.

Go back to *Spread Your Chest* (p. 126), and practice the exercise with this new awareness of tightness in your chest. This exercise creates the enhanced mobility in your shoulders that will enable you to join with the power of the horse so that he can't jerk his head down to pull you forward.

You have tremendous power in the subtle rotation of the humerus bone in your upper arm. With your humerus rotated, you enable the force from the reins to be passed through your arm, into the latissimus dorsi, and down to your seat. Rather than tightening your upper body and leaning back on the reins, just use a slight rotation of your upper arm. (See anatomical diagrams in the *Appendix*, p. 245.)

Root Causes

The root cause of many down-transition problems is bracing in the torso. First observe yourself carefully; do you tighten in this way? If so, keep track of the rhythm of your breath. Focus on breathing and relaxing so that you stay connected with your horse.

Revisiting the Trot

To ride the trot—sitting or posting, collected or lengthened—you apply the knowledge you've gained at the walk. The mechanics of the horse's two-beat gait affects your position and the way in which you ride.

At the trot, think of your spine moving like a flag in the wind. The flag moves in rolls as the force of the wind passes *through* it. When you have relaxed control of your joints, your limbs can stay still and sensitive as your spine rolls and moves with the energy of the horse. In Tai Chi, this is the principle of yield and overcome.

Before You Mount

Practice *Wall Sitting* (p. 59), in which you push your lower back into the wall. That same feeling should lead the sitting phase of your posting trot.

If we look at the movement and rhythm of the pelvis at the rising trot, we can say that it's two-beat: 1-up, 1-down; 1-up, 1-down. Your pelvis is in the saddle only every other beat. Once you sit the trot, your pelvis's rhythm doubles, as you must absorb every beat. To help you sit better, you need to relax all the muscles that you were using to balance and move yourself while posting.

Step-by-Step

1 While at the trot you want to engage your lower lumbar to help you sit straight and strong. When sitting, if you expand your lower back, opening the Ming Meng gate, you can maintain your connection with your horse (see "correct" photo).

For many riders, their main problem in the trot is their inability to surrender the spine fully to the motion of the horse. Usually a closed Ming Meng and a tight, braced lower back are the root causes. Many riders end up with a lower back braced in an accentuated arch, which cuts their body in half energetically. Rather than allowing the energy of the horse to move freely up their spine, the energy meets resistance in their lower or middle back. This resistance causes the upper part of their body to become unstable as the full force of the horse pushes against the resistance.

Your goal is to allow the lower lumbar to move. Use your mind and breath to soften your lower back.

At the posting trot, most riders do not sit truly straight and erect during the sitting phase. Their upper body is nearly always leaning slightly forward, and this misalignment prevents their bones from transferring energy through their bodies in relaxation (see "incorrect" photo). For instance, gravity still pulls the rider down, but due to this misalignment, the force doesn't travel into their seat to make their seat aids powerful. Without a deep connection in the seat, they resort to overusing their legs as a means of gaining impulsion in the horse.

The root of power for your legs, however, is not your seat, but your lower back. You must tighten your lower back to use your legs. Now your lower back becomes even tighter and your seat even more disconnected, and your position deteriorates even further into tension. As you can see, holding the lower back has a snowballing effect and it traps you in a weakened position.

2 When you are posting and you begin to drop your seat to the saddle, expand your lower back. Look ahead, imagining something in the sky like a soaring hawk or a string of balloons. Ride to the hawk or balloons. Allow your crown to float upward. And smile!

Step 1: Correct (left): the rider's lower lumbar is released and moving freely with the force of the horse, resulting in harmony and smooth, rhythmic motion. (Note: the rider's head position is too forward— a remnant of her compensatory mechanism to counterbalance her formerly closed back that will disappear as the rider next learns to open her crown.)

Incorrect (right): this rider's misalignment (leaning forward) locks the lower back, closes the Ming Meng, and the horse's energy enters the rider's body percussively, resulting in disharmony, unbalance, and a jolting ride.

Ride to the Balloons

One of the biggest challenges many riders have is keeping their heads up and their eyes off the horse. Looking down puts the head and neck in a weak and unhealthy position as far as structural balance is concerned. In this position, it is impossible to maintain the fluid rhythm of the spine while riding. With the head down, you must hold it balanced with the muscles of the neck and upper back, creating tension in the neck and shoulders of not only the rider, but the horse. To break this habit of looking down, I ask the rider to imagine a string of balloons floating in the air approximately 15 feet ahead of them. I ask them to tell me how many balloons are in the bunch and what colors they are. Look up and forward—ride to the balloons.

This visualization helps you focus on something other than your horse and it engages your imagination and intent. Experiment with it; play with it. See if it helps you place your head in the right position through relaxation rather than direct muscular effort.

3 When you are posting and you begin to drop your seat to the saddle, then your Ming Meng gate should expand and soften. Breathe in, expanding your lower back. This acts to release the muscle holding your spine. Yes, it's easier said than done, I know. You can apply the technique of counting the cadence at the trot to help in the timing of letting go with your lower back.

4 As you sit more erect, you can sit longer and deeper, so your horse really lifts you into the next posting phase. When you rise, lead the motion of your body using your awareness of opening your Dain Tian. In my mind, as I'm riding the posting trot, I experience a series of openings and closings of the Dain Tian and Ming Meng.

To help in the timing and rhythm at the trot, it may also be helpful to think of it in terms of *follow—match—lead*. When the horse lifts you, you are following. You rise and near the top of the motion, you've matched the rhythm. You sit and make contact with the saddle, and you lead. The cycle is then repeated throughout the trot.

Remember it is most effective to give aids when you are leading, which also means that your horse is following.

5 To build the energy of your trot, take deeper and quicker breaths. You're changing your intent, toward bigger and rounder strides. Your horse responds, so his strides become deeper and stronger, bigger and rounder.

You can also drive the horse by "bouncing" your breath off the ground. Visualize sending your breath down through the horse into the ground, when it then rebounds to you up through the horse's energized motion.

6 When you near the corner of the ring, expand your crown and lean from your lower lumbar. This is the same feeling as in *Hold the Sky with Both Hands* (p. 138). You should feel more weight on your inside seat bone. Your weight shifts and cues your horse to turn.

Opening the Gates

To help your trot work, you open these four gates: the Dain Tian, Ming Meng, Front of the Heart, and Back of the Heart. Opening the gates allows the energy of the horse to move through you without creating resistance.

> *Rider Insight, Margaret:* "I asked James if he could show me how I could encourage my horse to increase his suspension. He said to open up and receive his energy and movement. When I did this at the top of his stride (uppermost moment of suspension), it encouraged his back to lift, which created a definite increase in suspension and softness in my horse. The idea of receiving his energy rather than manipulating it was astronomically effective. Of course much of the reason that I could understand and execute James's instructions was due to our earlier unmounted work. The opening of the heart, front and back, greatly increased my capacity to feel the horse."

The Dain Tian and Ming Meng are directly responsible for maintaining a deep and active seat. They form the foundation necessary to open the heart. Opening the heart makes room for and invites the horse up into you. As you explore the relationship between opening and closing these gates and the movement of your horse, remember that it all starts with your breath and your intent.

The Constantly Changing Center

When riding, there is only one time that your weight should remain distributed 50/50 left and right in your seat: when your horse is at the halt with his feet square and parallel. At all other times, when the horse is moving, your weight is constantly shifting. Your center is actually a sphere that is constantly moving and changing. Trying to hold fast to a point that we call the center is impossible. To define your center you need to know where the outside edges lie.

Buddha said that entire answers lie in the middle ground—and to know the middle you must know the edges.

To enhance your balance, you want to redefine your outside edges and bring them closer together. In Tai Chi, as in riding, your balance cannot depend on a stationary position. It must be alive and moving—and always within your center.

Realize that the horse's center is also moving with the forward motion of the trot. To keep your centers joined, you pass through the center where both of you meet. When you ride in a posting trot imagine yourself passing through the center with each stride, so you're not trying to hold your center still. Think of letting your center breathe.

Exercises that you can use to open these gates and enhance your trot work include:
- *Open the Ming Meng* (p. 99)
- *Thrust Palm in Bow Stance* (p. 146)
- *Bend with an Arch* (p. 154)
- *Hip Circles* (p. 142)
- *Lift a Single Iron Arm* (p. 158)

All these exercises help you soften your lower lumbar and gain enhanced mobility in your spine. By practicing these exercises, you will be able to more reliably open your gates.

Reminder

If you tighten up those muscles around your spine, you won't be able to stay flexible enough to stay connected to your horse and his motion. Your seat will be weakened, and you will need to overuse your muscles to maintain your position. Because of your resulting rigidity, you won't be able to take advantage of the natural power that originates in your center. You then make up for this weakness by relying on more leg aids and spurs, because your horse is not getting the message from your seat.

The structural aspects of the trot relate back to *Sitting Meditation*. When your horse stands immobile, you can sit and focus on the awareness you gained in that exercise. See how opening your Ming Meng helps your horse move up into you.

Root Causes

Here is a list of symptoms that I see at the trot:

- Your head pushes forward or is constantly looking down.
- Your elbows are out and up.
- Your seat is bouncing, and your legs swing.
- You grip with your legs.
- Your upper body is not quiet.
- Your horse is constantly tugging on the reins.
- You must use your legs to keep the horse moving forward.

All these symptoms derive from a single root cause: an inability to move the lower lumbar region of the spine independently of the rest of the spine or the lower body. This inflexibility prevents the rider from having a connected seat. This lack of ability is apparent if you need to lean your upper body backward or forward to enhance the use of your seat. Leaning gives you leverage, and this extra power may make you feel safe. However, leaning also reduces your sensitivity to the movement of the horse—the connection that you seek.

Bending on the Circle

Whenever you bend your horse on a circle, turn him on the forehand, or turn him on the haunches, you can apply the tools of mind, breath, and body. Technically, to bend your horse, you move either your left or right seat bone forward. Moving the left seat bone forward bends the horse to the left; moving the right seat bone forward bends the horse to the right. This bends the horse but does not mean that he moves on a circle.

On the circle, you must shift your weight slightly to the inside seat bone. This causes your horse to step under your shifted center and move on the circle. If this is not the procedure you follow to ride a circle or turn a corner, chances are you need to apply an inside rein aid on every stride. You probably also find it necessary to keep your outside leg slightly back and on the horse to prevent the haunches from drifting out. All this activity makes for a very busy rider and a distracted horse. Once again, all these are symptoms of the root cause of not moving from your center.

Before You Mount

Earlier, I introduced moving your center from your belly button. Let's revisit that feeling, so you can transfer it to the saddle. You'll do less and get more response from your horse.

1 Sit in a hard, flat chair so that you feel your seat bones against the seat. Your feet should be flat on the ground; let your elbows rest at your sides.

2 Try moving your right seat bone forward, as if you were going to bend your horse. Was the motion effortless? Or did you struggle to find the muscles to move your seat bone?

3 Try it again, and listen closely to your body to determine what muscles you had to engage to move that seat bone forward.

Chances are one or more of these things happened:

- you had to pull with one leg and push with the other, causing one knee to move forward and one back;
- you pushed with the gluteus muscles and pulled with the abdominals—and in doing so, you tightened your lower back and abdomen.

4 Try it yet again, and consider these questions.

- When you moved your seat bone, did your weight remain equal in each seat bone?
- Did you lift one side of your body in order to lighten the seat bone that you wanted to move?
- Did you lean back to the left to move the right seat bone?
- Did your head and chest stay still or move forward instead of your seat bone?

Remember that moving your seat bone forward bends the horse.

As you investigate your movements, remember that you probably move in the same way in the saddle, whether you're aware of it or not—it's an established movement habit, one that we're trying to retrain and improve. If your habit includes any tension or unbalancing, remember too that your horse has to compensate for these problems.

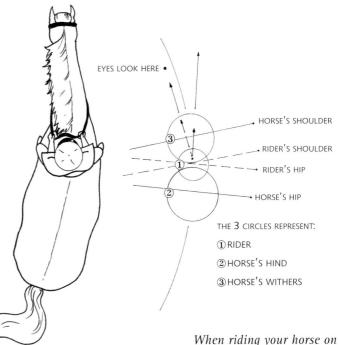

EYES LOOK HERE

HORSE'S SHOULDER
RIDER'S SHOULDER
RIDER'S HIP
HORSE'S HIP

③
①
②

THE 3 CIRCLES REPRESENT:
① RIDER
② HORSE'S HIND
③ HORSE'S WITHERS

When riding your horse on a circle, your shoulders should be aligned with the horse's shoulders, and your hips should be aligned with the horse's hips.

5 Once again, move your left seat bone forward, but this time do it by turning your belly button to the *right* (the outside of your imagined circle). As your left seat bone moves forward, you'll also notice that your right seat bone moves back. Keep your seat bones equally weighted (50/50). And keep your feet flat on the ground and your spine upright and relaxed.

Follow the path of mind, breath, and body. Focus your mind on your center. Relax your abdomen and let your breath expand the Dain Tian and Ming Meng.

6 Now reverse—that is, turn your waist (belly button/center) to the left, and notice that your right seat bone moves forward. You've just reversed your horse's bend.

7 Once again, listen again to your body as you make these moves. What muscles did you use to move? Did you feel the same tension as you did the first time I asked you to move your seat bone forward? Isn't it easier to turn your belly button than move your seat bone forward?

Bending on the Circle (cont.)

Practice this motion in the chair until you can move, breathe, and feel your center with ease. Your goal is a relaxed reorientation to the outside of your center—from which all motion comes—in order to move your inside seat bone forward, thereby bending your horse to the inside. Also important in this exercise is keeping your shoulders quiet, relaxed and independent of your center.

The drawing on page 199 illustrates the important goal you are aiming for: orient your shoulders and hips independently of each other, but in alignment with the horse's hips and shoulders. *When riding your horse on the circle or through a corner, your hips should match the horse's hips, and your shoulders match the horse's shoulders.*

Step-by-Step

1 When you mount, begin in *Sitting Meditation*. Complete your normal warm-up.

2 Walk your horse on a straight line. To move the horse onto a circle you are going to do two things, which are entirely independent of one another: you are going to *bend the horse from your center* (turning your belly button to what will be the outside of the circle), and *shift your weight into the seat bone you moved forward* (the inside seat bone).

3 To prove the independence of these two aids to yourself, move your right seat bone forward (by turning your center, your belly button, to the left) *while keeping the weight evenly distributed in your two seat bones.* Your horse will bend to the right but should continue to travel forward in a straight line.

4 Next, shift your weight slightly into the right (forward) seat bone. Your horse, already bent to the right, should now start to circle to the right as well. The most effective way to shift your weight without tensing is by leaning with a straight spine, just as you did in the exercise *Hold the Sky with Both Hands* (p. 138).

Weighting one seat bone or the other causes the horse to step under your now shifted center. This weighting creates the circle—not the bending. Weighting makes it easy for the horse, and it's the kindest thing you can do. He won't have to work against himself, trying to walk a circle in which you are pulling on the inside rein every stride to remind him to keep his head to the inside.

To ride an integrated, coherent circle, with rider and horse joined, do the following:

- Point your belly button to the outside (bringing your inside seat bone forward) to bend your horse to the inside; and,
- shift your weight slightly to the inside seat bone by leaning to the inside with a straight spine. (The leaning movement is subtle: your nose should move 2 inches or less to the inside; try to move it only one-half inch!) And,
- align your shoulders to match your horse's shoulders.

5 Check your alignment: you and your horse align corresponding body parts. Just think: *shoulders to shoulders; hips to hips.* Are your shoulders relaxed and aligned with your horse's? If not, relax, breathe, and let them align. (It's at moments such as this that all your groundwork pays off handsomely.)

6 As you continue to walk on a circle, project your intent forward and a little to the inside of your horse.

7 Pick up a trot. Imagine me standing in the center of your circle. Look at me while you keep your belly button turned away from me.

Move your seat without tightening your abdomen, seat, or legs. Move from the inside, using your internal muscles, and don't think about the seat bones. In this position your pelvis is free to move with the horse. This relaxed position also frees your legs to move independently, allowing you to give aids in rhythm with the horse's movements.

How did your horse respond? Remember, he's your professor, your best teacher. Most horses will lower their head and turn easily. The horse's spine does bend. He won't need a constant rein aid because he has truly bent through his whole body, not just moved his head to the inside.

In the beginning, it's easier to move your head and chest to the outside with your belly button, turning your whole body as one unit. But on the horse, you'll have to bring your head and shoulders into alignment with the horse's shoulders while maintaining the position of the belly button to the outside of the circle.

Opening the Gates

While riding on the circle, keep the Dain Tian and Ming Meng open. This requires a lot of practice on the ground and in the saddle in order to be able to do this effortlessly.

Pointing your belly button is the most effective and effortless way to move one seat bone forward and the other one back. Moving your belly button takes very little muscle effort, because you turn from your center. Your legs are relaxed, your gluteus muscles soft, and your abdomen and lower back relaxed. In this position, you can effectively follow the rhythm of the horse and adhere to all the previous principles and natural laws.

Your seat bones are fused together by your pelvis. They are like opposite spokes on a wheel. A balanced, efficient, and even way of moving them both is to move your center, which is like moving the hub of the wheel to move the spokes.

If you turn your center with your first two gates closed, you will close the heart gates, which will, in turn, cause the upper body to tense, bringing your chest, shoulders, and head to the outside.

> *Rider Insight, Linda: "At first I didn't get the idea of turning the belly button. After a little bit of practice I was amazed at how easily my horse was moving on the circle. His head was low and I could feel his back moving up into my seat. It was like riding on a big, soft ball. Leading with my belly button into corners has made all the difference in the world in staying 'through' in the corners."*

Reminder

Your goal is to turn—to move your seat bones—without affecting the structural alignment of your spine. You free up the push and pull in your legs, and release the push of gluteus muscles and the pull of abdominal muscles, which work in pairs. You also free up your lower back and open the Ming Meng. Guard against unconsciously tightening up your lower back.

Root Causes

The biggest challenge in turning your belly button is to turn *only* your belly button—keeping your shoulders still. If you can't do this on the ground, you won't be able to do it in the saddle, so practice on the ground. Repeat the unmounted portion of this exercise—Before You Mount on page 198, and practice *Thrust Palm in Bow Stance* (p. 146) to help you gain this mobility.

Canter

With its three-beat count and huge forward motion, the canter produces the greatest amount of energy of all the gaits we will work with in this book. The suspension, rise, and drop inherent in the movement of the horse's center will provide the best opportunity for you to practice your newly acquired skills.

The circular force and the slower, deeper rhythm of the canter makes it possible to feel as if you are riding *inside* your horse's center. As your centers join, you will feel the energy of the horse through your body and be challenged to redirect it through your gates.

My Riding Insight: While being longed at the canter on my trainer's very wonderful stallion, I first felt the concept of follow—match—lead.

It was as if time had slowed down and I was moving in a quiet stillness, feeling every footfall of my partner. My trainer observed that our breaths became synchronized. I began to let go of the tension in my body. As I did so, the horse began to fill up into me. I could feel the power of the horse moving through every gate in my body. I was reminded by my trainer to smile, and as I did it opened the Upper Pass and Crown gates in my head. With these gates open, I needed only to think the circle bigger and it got bigger. As I thought of collection, the horse collected. We had achieved a connection that I had only heard of before. (It's important to note that at that time I had only been riding for two years, and hadn't ridden at all for about five months.)

It was just about this time that I felt the horse drop out from under me as if he had stepped in a huge hole. I wasn't sure what had happened, and we continued to canter. My trainer seemed concerned and began to reel us in on the longe line. What had happened was that the horse had bucked and kicked.

In reviewing the video, the horse's hind feet were nearly as high as my head when he kicked. However, in this state of oneness, with all my gates open, I was able to stay effortlessly connected to his center through all his movements, including the bucking. This is a state that you, too, can ride in.

I don't intend to teach a "how-to-canter" lesson. The lesson will be "how to become one at the canter."

Before You Mount

Review *Smooth, Invisible Transitions* (p. 183). You're going to re-enter that giant bubble.

Let's also briefly review the horse's three-beat movement in the canter:

- On the first beat, the horse steps under with his outside hind and propels himself (and you) up and forward.
- In the second beat, the diagonal pair (inside hind and outside fore) comes through, further lifting horse and rider toward the apex of the motion, which occurs between the second and third beats.
- On the third beat, the inside fore comes through, sending the horse into the suspension phase, during which his body falls to its lowest point before beginning to rise again with the first beat of the next stride.

Step-by-Step

1 When you mount, begin in *Sitting Meditation*. Complete your normal warm-up.

2 Ride your best walk or trot right through its last stride before the transition to canter. The quality of your canter depends on your transition. Use your intent to project yourself into the canter as you did earlier in the walk-trot transition. Visualize that large bubble where the canter is already happening, and flow into the transition.

I think of the beginning of the canter is like taking off on a large wave or dropping over the edge of a very steep ski run. If you hesitate in your body or mind, you will be left behind from the very start and have to play catch-up with a very large energy. That's not an easy task.

To examine my first analogy, think of riding a canter as if you were going to ride a 10-foot ocean wave. If your weight is slightly back and the canter starts big, you will be left behind. In an attempt to catch up, you'll probably arch your back and push your hips forward. This, in turn, causes you to tighten your abdomen and hold your breath. This tension is immediately transferred to the horse, who often falls out of the canter because of it. Don't inhale and hold your breath.

3 Take a deep breath and exhale. Your breath tells the horse that you are changing.

4 When you enter the sphere of the transition, you should be inhaling deep into the belly with the Dain Tian and Ming Meng open. Open the Back of the Heart gate, expanding your shoulder blades. Your chest should be soft and slightly dropped with your armpits empty.

5 Ask for the canter with your leg, paying close attention to your abdomen. Keep it relaxed, soft and following as your horse picks up the canter.

6 On the second canter beat, you continue to feel the energy rise from the hindquarters of the horse. Allow it to enter your body through the Ming Meng and travel up into the Back of the Heart, and then to the Front of the Heart.

7 At this point your horse's back will start to drop away. Again, maintain that relaxed, soft center whose expansion and stretching will allow you to follow the horse's back as it drops down from your center.

8 As the horse's inside fore comes through, you enter the suspension phase. During this phase, the Front of the Heart should be completely open. Opening this gate helps to project your intent forward and keep your body light and balanced.

9 Before the horse begins the next canter stride, exhale and drop the energy in your heart down your front to the Dain Tian and back to the horse. You are now ready to repeat the cycle.

Receive the force of the horse through your lower back, let it move into the upper body, and then fall back down your front, where it returns to your horse. This circulation of the horse's energy will help keep you from hollowing your lower back. Some hollowing—emptying of the lower back—is natural, but too much acts to cut your body in half energetically, preventing the flow of energy between you and your horse. Your upper body falls out of rhythm with your center and the horse. In addition, a hollowed back makes you rigid, and this causes your falling motion to end in collision with the horse's back. This impact discomforts and unbalances the horse, as well as disconnects you, making it all the harder for you to join the horse's rising motion which has already begun as he completes the suspension phase and begins the next canter stride.

10 Breathe and relax as the next canter stride begins. Maintain your posture and send you and your horse forward with your clear, focused intent.

11 If you're cantering on a circle, be sure to turn your belly button to the outside to bend your horse effortlessly.

When you are cantering on a circle, the horse's increased speed creates a much stronger sense of centripetal force than you felt on a similar size circle at the trot. Instead of getting caught up in the tension of "trying to stay on," simply relax and turn your belly button to the outside to stay with your horse. Turning in this way—bending from your center—also places both your legs in a perfect inside-forward and outside-back position.

If your horse is not really bent, you will have to use the inside rein at least once in every stride. As the horse's inside front leg impacts the ground and begins to transfer his force forward by pushing off, his head and neck will try to straighten if the spine is not bent. This is when you will pull with the rein to bring his head back on the circle. This constant focus on the rein creates tension in your arm and shoulder and causes the Chi Who gate on that side to close. The result inhibits the sensitivity of your hand and creates tension in your upper body.

Reminder

Tension in your body gives outside forces of gravity, momentum, and centripetal force something to "push" against. Instead employ these forces as your allies in the canter by aligning your bones, deepening your breath, and connecting to the rhythm of your horse. This allows you to relax and let energy flow through you, just as an ocean wave's tremendous energy passes quietly through open water but becomes a crashing, violent force when it meets resistance, such as a shoreline. Be like the water. If you carry tension in your body, you become like the shoreline, and all these allies become opponents.

Opening the Gates

Cantering involves opening all the Eight Gates. You know that the first four gates—the Dain Tian, Ming Meng, and the Back and Front of the Heart—are first on the list to open. They are truly your foundation. To connect completely with the bigger energy of the canter, it is also necessary to open the Upper Pass, Crown, and Chi Who gates.

While the Chi Who (left and right) are opened primarily by softening the chest and emptying the armpits, you open the Upper Pass and Crown more through your intent than any physical action. Smiling and suspending the crown are the keys that unlock the gate, but your intent pushes it open.

Up until now I haven't addressed Gate 6: The Liver and Spleen. The dropping of the horse's back at the canter is an ideal time to feel the Liver and Spleen gate opening and closing. When the horse drops away, you allow your abdomen to stretch. When your pelvis drops, following the horse's back, the Liver and Spleen gate opens. If you do not squeeze with your abdominal muscles when your horse lifts you up, your gates stay open. The rolling motion of the canter can have a massaging effect on your internal organs if these gates remain soft and open.

When you ride with Gate 6 open, your horse's forehand becomes incredibly light and responsive. You can feel the front feet of your horse as if there were a string connecting each hoof with your gut.

Exercises that help at the canter include:

- *Walking Backward* (p. 62)
- *Open the Ming Meng* (p. 99)
- *Hip Circles* (p. 142)
- *Spread Your Wings* (p. 131)
- *Hold the Sky with Both Hands* (p. 138)
- *Thrust Palm in Bow Stance* (p. 146)

Root Causes

Problems that I see at the canter include:
- Riders brace in the upper body.
- Riders bounce in the seat.
- Riders hold their abdomen tight and bear down. Their breath shortens and comes up high into the chest. The shoulder blades pinch together, and the chin comes down and in toward the chest. They lean the upper body (not the full, straight spine) to the inside of the cantering circle, so they're not structurally aligned to deal with the centripetal force of the horse's motion.

All these symptoms derive from not maintaining a balanced, connected center with your horse.

Tai Chi at the Horse Show

One of the great side benefits of developing the path of mind, breath, and body is how the skills you gain can help you at shows and performances—anywhere those butterflies end up in your stomach. Try to remember the last time you competed in a dressage test, rode in an exposition, or performed in front of a crowd. Did you feel anxious? Do you know why you were nervous?

My Riding Insight: Perhaps you're a bit like me—the moment before I'm "on," I wonder if I should be performing. Did I skip a day of training? Am I sufficiently prepared? Thoughts like these are unproductive and can in no way enhance your performance. The only thing they do is take you out of the present moment and distract you from your body and breath.

During my martial arts career I had the opportunity to perform publicly at least four times a year for fourteen years. While working a full-time job and practicing my art six days a week, four to six hours a day after work, I often ran out of time to practice the extra forms for demonstration. So, I began practicing in my head; I would go through the entire form, motion by motion in my mind, usually at my lunch break or before I went to sleep at night.

The problem with this practice was that a form that might take ten minutes to complete in real time would take only seconds in my head. I realized that I was only thinking about the form, not actually doing it. As a result, when I returned to physically practicing the form, I would find myself arriving at moments when I didn't know whether or not I had just left out a huge piece of the form. If I didn't think at all, it was fine—I had done the forms so many times that my body knew what to do regardless of whether or not my mind was present. In some martial arts, achieving this state of "no mind" is a good thing, but in Tai Chi it is not, in which the goal is complete mind–body connection. I had to come up with another mental rehearsal technique.

My solution was to continue to practice in my mind, but to move in concert with my breath, so that I was doing the form in real time instead of just thinking about it. I realized two things while working this way: (1) I could not stay focused through the whole form without being distracted by some random thought; and (2) there were times that I held my breath, usually just prior to difficult motions or motions that I did not fully understand. These were both valuable experiences: the former taught me that my concentration needed to improve, and the latter pointed out to me just what sections I needed to work on. While somewhat painful to encounter, our weaknesses always give us our greatest learning opportunities.

This type of mental practice is an invaluable self-teaching method. Try it the next time you're going to compete.

Sit at the in-gate of the arena or wherever you're going to perform. In your mind's eye see yourself perform the entire test, jumping round, or pattern.

Breathe yourself through from start to finish. Do you start by inhaling or exhaling? Where is your breath when you ride right in front of the judge? Make that transition? Begin the tempi changes? Halt and salute? Are you smiling, or is your face tense? Are you clenching your jaw? Envision the performance as fully as possible.

Repeat your mind's eye performance, noting your start time.

When you are done, note the time, determine how long your "performance" took, and compare this time to the actual performance time. Ask yourself, "Did I get distracted? Where did I hold my breath? Did I speed up through sections that I do not completely understand or that I find difficult?"

I have found that this type of practice actually improved my performances more quickly than just repeating the physical motions over and over. Until you can do your test, course, or pattern in your mind in real time, you don't know the routine through and through. This technique is invaluable in getting off a learning plateau and reaching the next level in understanding yourself and your art.

Lateral Movements

The same techniques and abilities you learned to bend your horse are also used to perform lateral movements such as leg-yield, shoulder-in, and half-pass. The one change is that you don't hold your center (your belly button) in a static position—instead, it moves rhythmically with your horse. You need flexible, independent control of your shoulders and pelvis, as you need to align your shoulders with the horse's shoulders and your hips with the horse's hips. The exercise *Thrust Palm in Bow Stance* (p. 146) is extremely helpful for gaining this mobility.

In lateral work, your center is your primary aid, and your leg is the support aid. They work in harmony with each other. You lead with your center, follow with your leg, allow the horse to move through, and follow the horse. This all happens within one stride, and you repeat the process in the next stride. The movement of your center feels like an oblong figure eight, with the bigger side moving in the direction the horse is going (see drawing).

The principle of *follow—match—lead* is never more apparent than it is here.

The opening and closing of Gate 6: The Liver and Spleen strongly affects the fluidity and "throughness" of this technique. The opening of the gate leads you into and through the motion.

Opening the Gates

Allow the Liver and Spleen gate to soften and expand so that energy flows from the hind end of the horse through your torso and back into the horse's forehand. It is common for riders to resist the force coming from the horse at their rib cage. This happens when they tighten their upper abdominal muscles as the force pushes up into their torso. The result is excess movement in the upper body, which in turn means that their upper body tenses and resists the horse's movement. This creates imbalance in the rider that causes further tensing, and it interferes with the horse's motion.

As in the canter, it is impossible to open Gate 6: The Liver and Spleen gate if the Front and Back of the Heart gates are not already open. The liver and spleen are located below your ribs, on either side of your body. You open Gate 6 by letting go with your upper abdominal muscles and allowing the force of the horse's step to move through your body. The muscles involved are both involuntary and voluntary. By breathing deep into the belly, you let go of the voluntary muscles. The movement of the horse will aid in relaxing the involuntary muscles. Rarely in your everyday life do you think about using these muscles. They open when you laugh, and they slam shut when you cough or sneeze.

You can also open Gate 6 through massage. When open, the outer muscles are soft, so you can push your fingers into your body under your rib cage. Your diaphragm is up inside there. You can feel it push down and out if you breathe into the Dain Tian.

Your seat receives the horse's energy through the open Ming Meng. Your seat then redirects this energy out either the Liver (right) or Spleen (left) gate, depending on your direction. If you leg-yield to the left, you receive most of the horse's power up through your right seat bone. It's transferred through the Ming Meng diagonally through your center and then into your spleen (left) gate. The energy is then sent out through the opened gate and projected back into the horse. It's a circular motion, a flow of energy. Use your intent to lead with the open gate in the direction you're moving. With practice, you can refine this work, opening and closing the Ming Meng to create a half-halt that's accomplished primarily with your breath.

The figure-eight movement of energy in lateral work

If you have a dominant side—and for many riders this is their right side—you must surrender it. For example, if you're right dominant, you need to open the left gate and project the energy through, thereby pulling your right side through. Similarly, your intent moves your body and your horse, and it too pulls you through, instead of pushing.

Jumping

Your center and the horse's center should match in the air over a fence. To achieve this harmony, in the takeoff imagine propelling your center over the fence. Use the same strategy that you used to create smooth and effortless transitions; that is, use your *intent.* By creating and seeing in your mind's eye the perfect jump, and then projecting it to a sphere that encompasses the entire jump area, you will be able to focus (mind) on your timing (breath) and your balance (body).

Step-by-Step

1 When you approach a jump, ask yourself whether or not you are inhaling or exhaling, or even holding your breath. Remember that your breathing sets your rhythm, and rhythm is the key to perfect timing.

2 In working with jumpers of various skill levels, I've found that the most effective breathing pattern is to inhale as the horse begins to drop his force into the ground, just prior to pushing off. This is a good example of "the root of lightness is heaviness."

3 As the horse and you leave the ground, start the exhaling and continue until just before landing on the other side.

4 Inhale as you land. Remember to breathe deep into your abdomen, opening the Dain Tian and Ming Meng.

If you allow your breath to stay up in your chest, you create a very high center away from your horse's center. Chest breathing is a bit like strapping a 20-pound weight to your chest and then trying to jump. In addition, if you hold your breath while jumping, it locks your body into a rigid position and decreases your ability to stay in balance with your horse. Such imbalance causes heavier landings that are hard on both bodies.

Eventually, you will be able to breath in this way over jumps effortlessly and unconsciously, and your connection with your horse will be sustained throughout your jumping round. At this point, you may then start to project your intent out beyond the jump itself.

5 To start, pick a point well past the jump to keep your eyes focused on—perhaps 20 to 30 yards out. If that is not possible because of a turn in the course, then focus on where the upcoming turn will take place.

When I work in person with someone, I stand 20 yards beyond the jump and have the rider keep eye contact with me as she approaches, jumps, and lands. The whole time we both smile and keep our hearts open. The resulting jumps are typically quiet and light.

Opening the Gates

In jumping it's essential that you open the Ming Meng, Front and Back of the Heart, Crown, and Upper Pass gates, and you need to project your intent forward. Jumping is the ultimate realization of "where the mind goes the body follows." More than any other form of riding, jumping demands lightness and thoroughness.

A balanced jumping seat demands that your pelvis be pushed back slightly. In this position, your lower back and thighs support more of the weight of your body. You can use your lower back without becoming tense and rigid. Avoid rigidity by keeping your breath down and the Ming Meng open, so you allow the energy of the horse to move up through you as he jumps.

Reminder

Remember that any resistance to the flow of energy is actually pushing against it. Such resistance is oftentimes the root cause of back pain in jumpers. With the Ming Meng open, the Back of the Heart can be open during the jump. You'll keep your upper body light, which in return will minimize the possibility of your weight crashing into the horse's forehand upon landing. Notice that the gates we are focusing on—Ming Meng, Heart, Crown, Upper Pass—all open upward during a jump and help to create suspension in your body. You'll float with your horse over the fence.

Practical Physics: Negotiating Centripetal Force

Earlier in the book we briefly discussed centripetal force (p. 11), the potentially unbalancing lateral force you experience whenever you turn or ride a circle. Now I'd like to revisit this subject and explain the forces at play and show you how the skills you have been learning can help you compensate for these forces and ride better turns and circles.

Here's a more detailed summary of the physics involved:

1 Our starting point is inertia, the property Newton described in his First Law of

Motion: unless acted on by a force, objects in motion travel straight ahead at an unchanging speed, and objects at rest remain at rest.

2 A moving object's "quantity of motion" is called its momentum*.

3 Thus, we have moving objects, with measurable momentum, tending to travel straight ahead unless acted on by a force. If we use a moving car as an example, that force can be with the motion of the car (acceleration), against the motion of the car (braking), or lateral to the motion of the car (turning). The last of these is centripetal force.

4 When you apply centripetal (center-seeking) force to an object traveling in a straight line, the object's path is altered from straight ahead to ahead but at an angle.

If the centripetal force is maintained, these moments of the object moving forward at a small angle add up—first to produce a turn, and eventually to produce a full circle.

The "sharpness" of the turn and the size of the circle depend on the relative influences of momentum (the "quantity of motion" proceeding straight ahead) and centripetal force (pushing or pulling sideways on the object).

Returning to the example of the car, you know that the more sharply you turn the steering wheel, the more sharply the car turns. This is because the car's tires, when turned more sharply, push against the pavement at a greater angle, deflecting the car from its straight path to one forward at an angle. The tires push the car sideways, making it turn, and creating centripetal force.

When you're a passenger riding in the car your inertia (tendency to move straight forward) and momentum are constant—until the car turns. As the car turns left, for instance, you are "thrown" against the right door—in reality, your body keeps traveling straight ahead until it collides with the interior of the car, which is moving left. Once you're pressed against the passenger door, the car keeps pulling you left as it continues to turn; the car is exerting a centripetal force (force toward the center of the turn) on you.

To summarize: in a turn forward momentum is deflected from a straight line to forward at an angle by the application of lateral (centripetal) force.

5 Now, let's look at these same physics, but with you on your horse:

* Momentum (p) is defined as $p = mv$, that is, an object's momentum is its mass times its velocity.

a) First, your horse accelerates you from a standstill up to the speed of your chosen gait; from this you gain your forward motion, momentum, and inertia—the tendency to keep moving forward at the same speed and direction.

b) Second, when your horse turns he not only carries you forward, but also exerts a lateral, centripetal force on you, pushing you toward the circle's center a little bit with every stride. The horses hooves, pushing off against the ground at an angle, are like the car's turned tires. As a result, you and your horse move forward at an angle, and if you do this for a sufficient number of strides, you complete a circle.

6 Many riders, when asked about the forces they sense while riding a circle, report not that they feel centripetal force "pushing them to the inside," but rather that they are "falling to the outside." Why?

Inertia is a property of all moving objects and your body's tendency is always to move straight ahead. Because your horse is turning—moving forward at an angle—you and your horse are simply on diverging paths: he is moving forward and to the inside, and you are moving straight ahead, which, relative to your horse, is to his outside. As your horse "disappears" out from underneath you, you feel you are falling to the outside.

7 Two factors increase centripetal force: increasing your speed, and making the circle smaller. Practically speaking, most riders begin to notice centripetal force and inertia (even if they would not use these terms) when trotting a circle of 10 meters or less, or cantering a circle of 20 meters or less.

Regardless of the speed at which you sense these forces and what they "feel like" to you, the physical reality is that your body must negotiate both inertia and centripetal force when riding a turn or circle.

8 Given these physics, now let's look at the situation practically:

You're riding a circle, sitting in a saddle that's moving forward and pulling you to the inside, and your body as a whole is traveling straight forward. You can't ignore either force. How do you reconcile them physically? You can negotiate a physical compromise in many different ways—with ease or with a struggle.

Most of our instinctual responses are not helpful and they generally involve tension.

(Tension in your body is always an excellent clue; it's a signal that you're using an ineffective strategy.) These unproductive responses include:

- leaning into the turn
- collapsing the inside hip
- gripping with the legs
- hanging on the inside rein

All of these approaches have two unfortunate consequences to varying degrees: they disconnect you from your horse, and they cause your horse to compensate for you in ways that inhibit his movement.

As you know by now, on the mind–breath–body path we are following in our work, we always seek to move in concert with the principles of Tai Chi. We will, therefore, look for a relaxed, balanced solution: use the mind, not force; never oppose force with force; yield and overcome; balance like a scale; seek stillness in motion; be heavy and light; focus and expand.

You have far better options than tensing or struggling; use the tools you learned in *Bending on the Circle* (p. 198).

    a)   turn your belly button to the outside, bringing your inside seatbone forward and aligning your hips with the horse's hips;

    b)   shift your weight onto the inside seatbone;

    c)   align your shoulders with the horse's shoulders; and,

    d)   relax and use your body to join and balance these two alignments and the forces associated with each.

When you sit in this way, your body exhibits a fascinating wisdom from the standpoint of physics:

- by turning your belly button to the outside, you align your pelvis with your body's inertia, which always travels straight ahead, perpetually leaving the circle; and
- by turning your shoulders to the inside, you align them with the path you are traveling on with the horse, which is your momentum as deflected by centripetal force.

In short, your body is simultaneously aligned with both of the physical influences affecting you when you ride a circle! And because you are doing this in centered, balanced relaxation, you have achieved an artful compromise.

This "double-alignment" that you've accomplished is subtle when a rider is on a large circle; that is, the centripetal component is modest compared to your straight-line momentum, and your shoulders only need to shift a little to the inside.

If we watch a rider in a canter pirouette, however, we can more easily see these two forces at work because they are more nearly equal:

- the centripetal component is greatly increased because the radius of the pirouette is so small (decreasing the radius of a turn or circle increases the centripetal effect); and,
- the forward momentum of the rider is much less in the pirouette.

Responding to these two forces, the rider is now more visibly aligned in two different directions. The rider's shoulders are turned further to the inside of the rider's pelvis, sometimes so much so that the rider almost seems to be looking back over her inside shoulder.

Now when you watch other riders on a circle, look at the alignment of their pelvis versus their shoulders. Can you see these forces interacting? How are they using their bodies to negotiate these conflicting energies? Are they relaxed or tense? And don't forget to ask yourself all these same questions when you ride a circle.

These techniques don't negate centripetal force and momentum—nothing can—but they do allow you to respond in relaxation rather than with force. You align your bones to exactly balance the forces. Struggling against physics with muscular effort is replaced by going with the motion in relaxed alignment, which creates a base from which you have independent control of your legs, arms, and hands to guide your horse as needed with aids.

Summary

This chapter has pulled together information from the entire book. It asked you to use your breath with relaxed attention, to focus your mind with clear intent, and to move your body with enhanced mobility, and then draw all those abilities together to use them while riding. No set of instructions in this chapter is long, but as you can sense, you can spend a lifetime practicing them without boredom, without repetition—and

The greatest benefit derived from using your breath to gain access to your body and its hidden abilities is that it keeps you absolutely present in your body—and this presence is the basis of awareness, and it takes absolute awareness to retrain your body, create new habits, and leave behind old habits. Any distraction that diverts your awareness will allow an old habit to slip back in.

Being in the moment is of vital importance. You must practice keeping your focus on you, not the horse. This is not to say that you are not aware of what your horse is doing, quite the contrary. When you are completely present, all your senses are heightened, and you will be able to feel even the slightest change in your horse without ever having to look down.

If and when your horse acts up or does something that you did not ask for, do not automatically look down at your horse, as if that will change things or make him listen. Instead, ask yourself, "Did I have anything to do with my horse's action? Did I unknowingly hold my breath, or tighten somewhere in my body? Did I ask for this change?" This is not to say that your horse never misbehaves or acts entirely on his own, but we want to be clear on what our role may have been.

without perfection. Awareness, health, and joy are our ultimate goals—and what better partner could you have on this journey than your horse?

What's Next

In chapter 8, "The Road Continues: Health and Tai Chi," I will look in greater detail at the health benefits of practicing Tai Chi. In addition, I have included a section called "Frequent Questions and Answers," in which I share my answers to questions that I often hear in clinics.

The Road Continues

Health and Tai Chi

THE JOURNEY WE HAVE BEGUN IN THIS BOOK may suggest questions and areas for further study. Here, I'll share more information about how Tai Chi can improve your well-being, and also address some of the questions and concerns that I most often hear from riders.

Healing Aspects of Tai Chi

Tai Chi is a three-in-one exercise of the mind, chi (breath), and body. Chinese medicine, too, recognizes this same interrelationship of mind, chi, and body. The philosophy underlying traditional Chinese medicine asserts the importance of balancing various opposing, but complementary, natural forces or energies—Yin and Yang—in the macrocosm of the universe, as well as in the microcosm that is the human being. All illness and disease are seen as the result of an imbalance of these forces known as chi. Traditional Chinese medicine encompasses many techniques to balance chi in the body in order to attain health and longevity. Acupressure, acupuncture, herbal medicine, Tai Chi, chi gong, and a complete dietetic system all take this same integrated and balanced approach to creating and maintaining optimal health and spirituality.

In Chinese medicine the environment in which you live, the foods you eat, and the exercises you do are all essential to maintaining your health. There is a saying in Chinese medicine: "A healthy fish cannot long swim in dirty water."

This chapter addresses only a small part of the healing process of Chinese medicine. Tai Chi is no quick fix to your health problems. The environment of your body took a long time to pollute. It did not happen overnight, but over your lifetime. With earnest practice, proper movement of the body, and correct breathing, you can enhance your health.

You have used abdominal breathing to help lower your center of balance and connect the mind with the body. This type of breathing can also bring significant health gains, including an increased lung capacity that promotes the exchange of gases in the body. In addition, abdominal breathing acts as an internal massage of the organs of the visceral cavity, including the kidneys, stomach, bladder, colon, large and small intestine, liver, and spleen. The daily movement of these organs helps balance and maintain their health.

Studies in the U.S. and China show that the practice of Tai Chi promotes health of the nervous system due to the calming effect it has on the cerebral cortex. The cerebral cortex links all activities in the human body through the central nervous system. This effect can be beneficial in the control of chronic diseases such as hypertension and peptic ulcers. In addition, these calming effects ripple throughout the nervous system and beyond; studies have demonstrated that Tai Chi practice is linked to the reduction of chemicals responsible for the body's production of adrenaline (a precursor for heart disease), and a decrease in the levels of stored lactic acid.

My own teacher, Wen Mei Yu, was first directed to Tai Chi at the age of seventeen as a means of healing a chronic ulcer. Within nine months the ulcer was gone. There are numerous studies proving the beneficial effects of Tai Chi for various systems in the body. I encourage you to research on your own the many resources available for your particular needs. See the bibliography on page 252 for some suggested reading.

The healing effects of Tai Chi are inherent in its practice. In order to make these health gains you need not focus your attention on them. You will heal yourself by simply "doing" the practice. Create the time and space for your own practice. What more meaningful, more empowering gift could you possibly give yourself?

Motion Meditation

As a healing art, Tai Chi balances and promotes the flow of chi in the body. If there is a lack of chi (energy), the combination of movements, increased oxygen intake, and stimulation of the Dain Tian increases your vital energy. If you have an overabundance of chi up in the head, which may be seen as hyperactivity or compulsive thinking, the forms balance the chi and calm the mind. The flowing movements of the body directed by the mind create with practice what is known as "motion meditation." Just as the body's systems benefit from the therapeutic motion, the mind benefits from the calming effect of focusing exclusively on the form.

After a time of regular practice, you may feel as if your mind is actually observing your body's movement rather than dictating it. Often when I complete my Tai Chi practice I realize that I have completely lost my sense of time, and I'm not sure whether I have been practicing for one hour or three hours. This is not an *out-of-body* experience, but rather a completely *in-body* experience.

Troubleshooting Your Own Riding and Health

The human body needs to be moved and used within the laws of nature to sustain health. Many of the injuries we sustain are caused by either abuse (meaning literally "use that causes injury") or by trying to use the body without regard for the natural laws. For example, not warming up before you ride is an example of abuse, and using brute strength against a far stronger force (your horse) is an example of working outside the natural laws.

Below I will help you identify the possible root causes for a variety of injuries, symptoms, and problems common in riding. I provide short- and long-term solutions, referring you to exercises from the previous chapters that will be helpful in healing yourself or resolving the problem.

Riding Problems and Tai Chi Exercise Solutions

Lower back pain after riding

Possible Root Causes and Effects

Bracing in the abdomen and lower back abuses the small muscles in the lumbar region of the spine.

When you hold tension in your spine, it acts as a lever against the lower lumbar region and pelvis. This effect creates a tremendous amount of potentially damaging force.

Short Term Strategies

Exercises: *Hold the Sky with Both Hands; Horse Stance; Thrust Palm in Bow Stance; Bend with an Arch; Hip Circles*

Long Term Strategies

Keep the Ming Meng and Dain Tian gates open while riding. Always seek a rhythmic and fluid movement in your spine.

Neck or shoulder pain during or after riding

Possible Root Causes and Effects

Misalignment of the head over the neck.
Overdependence on the trapezius muscles for strength and balance in the upper body.

Short Term Strategies

Exercises: *Neck Turns; Lift a Single Iron Arm; Spread Your Wings; Spread Your Chest*

Long Term Strategies

Keep the Chi Who and Front and Back of the Heart gates open while riding. Learn to engage the latissimus dorsi muscles of your back while riding, to allow the force applied on your body to travel down the spine and into your seat back to the horse.

Holding your breath while riding

Possible Root Causes and Effects

Lack of balance; fear of falling; or bracing in the abdomen.

Short Term Strategies

Exercises: *Abdominal Breathing*; *Counting Your Breath*; *Open the Ming Meng*
Find your structural alignment in the saddle.

Long Term Strategies

At least three times a day become aware of your breath and take a deep abdominal breath. In other words, on a daily basis be mindful of your breath. Remember holding your breath is a symptom, and there is always a reason: look for the cause that *precedes* your holding it.

Constantly looking down at your horse to "see" if he's done what you've asked

Possible Root Causes and Effects

Misalignment of upper body over the center, causing your head to move forward to maintain balance.
Poor mind-body connection so you must "see to believe."

Short Term Strategies

Exercises: *Neck Turns; Lift a Single Iron Arm; Spread Your Chest; Sitting Meditation; Wrist Shaking; Side Step; Walking Backward*

Long Term Strategies

Use your mind to direct your body. Become aware of your peripheral vision and start to see more. Expand your awareness. Open Gate 8: The Crown and Gate 7: The Upper Pass. Smile and see the balloons.

Your lateral work on one side is significantly better than the other

Possible Root Causes and Effects

One side of the body is dominant over the other, and you are twisting or holding in the spine to compensate for imbalance.

Short Term Strategies

Exercises: *Hold the Sky with Both Hands; Hold Knee to Chest; Walking Backward; Wall Sitting*

Long Term Strategies

Practice, through abdominal breathing techniques, the opening and closing of Gate 6: The Liver and Spleen. Pay close attention to the role your mind plays in your body's left and right dominance. It's as though one side of the body takes over in an attempt to make up for the apparent weakness in the other side.

This role of dominance is often hard to let go of, even after the balance is returned. Is one side of your body not allowing the other side to lead?

If the right side is dominant, but it's now the left side's turn to lead, you may have to focus more on letting go with the right than leading with the left.

Your horse does not change gaits when you ask, or he takes a few strides to pick up the new gait

Possible Root Causes and Effects

Lack of intent.

Holding your breath as you enter the transition.

Lack of structural balance is making your aids unclear.

Short Term Strategies

Exercises: *Abdominal Breathing; Counting Your Breath; Walking Backward*
Review all the *Opening Your Gates* and *Intent* sections in chapter 7.

Long Term Strategies

Become aware throughout your day what you project. For example, do you project negative outcomes for future events, or do you hope for and expect the best? Are you sure your horse is going to spook at the place he "always" does before you get there?

Notice throughout the day how your intent affects your breathing. When you are anticipating a negative result, does your breath shorten and stay high in your chest?

Be sure you are not throwing away a good walk to make your transition to the trot. See *Smooth, Invisible Transitions* in chapter 7.

While riding on a circle you: (1) drift in or out from the circumference of the circle; (2) find yourself hanging or leaning off to one side or the other of the saddle; or (3) constantly need to use the inside rein to keep your horse's head on the circle

Possible Root Causes and Effects

Looking into the center of the circle without regard for the outside of the circle.

Leaning the upper body into the circle rather than actually bending the horse.

Using just the leg and rein to ride a circle.

Short Term Strategies

Exercises: *Embracing the Moon; Heaven and Earth*

Review *Practical Physics* (p. 213) and *Bending on the Circle* (p. 198).

Long Term Strategies

Practice leading by using Gate 6: The Liver and Spleen; if going to the left, use the spleen; if going to the right, use the liver.

Your horse does not track up at the walk or trot

Possible Root Causes and Effects

Bracing in the lower back.

Riding with Gates 3 and 4, the Front and Back of the Heart gates closed.

Not being in rhythm with the horse.

Any of these cause your center to move behind the center of the horse. Because your two centers are joined, if your center moves back, so does your horse's. In order to stay in balance he has to shorten his stride. The further you move the center back, the shorter his stride has to be.

A second reason that a horse may not track up is that your weight is slightly off-center to the left or the right. This condition will cause the horse's hoof to fall sooner under the side that is heavier. This is common while riding on a circle, although often overlooked.

Short Term Strategies

Exercises: *Open the Ming Meng; Embracing the Moon; Heaven and Earth; Walking Backward*

Review *Smooth, Invisible Transitions* (p. 183) and *Bending on the Circle* (p. 198)

Long Term Strategies

Keep Gate 8: the Crown; Gate 7: the Upper Pass; and Gates 3 and 4: the Heart gates open, and project your intent out and up. Look at the balloons, as described on page 194.

Make sure when riding on a circle that you allow your horse to bend and that you're not leaning to the inside of the circle more than necessary. See *Bending on a Circle* (p. 198).

Relieving Stress with Tai Chi

It is well known that stress is a killer—maybe more so than we truly understand. Stress enters the body through the mind. If it is not recognized and addressed at that moment, it will move into the body and find a home. Once in the body, it becomes much more difficult to dislodge and move out.

Stress of the mind becomes tension in the body. This tension seems to take up residence in the most fragile rooms in the body, such as the neck, spine, and lower back. It then begins to apply its force to the nerves, pushing and pulling until ultimately stopping you in your tracks.

I often think that the scenario described here is actually the body's last defense against a driven mind that pushes you forward, dragging the body along without regard for your well-being and needs. My good friend and mentor, Dr. Syng Ku Yu, founder of the International Finger Pressure Institute in Pomona, California, says there are three things needed for great health. In order of importance, these include (1) replenishing and rejuvenating sleep; (2) a healthy diet that includes more vegetables than meat; and (3) exercise. So, the number one factor in creating and maintaining health is quality sleep. The number one killer of quality sleep is stress.

In the East they say the body is your temple, and your mind is the main gate to the temple. Tai Chi addresses stress at the gate as well as in the temple. The slow, light, and relaxed movements of the whole body must be directed by the mind, not forced. This slow-motion dance requires and facilitates the brain's control and balance of the body. It is as if the body teaches the brain to slow down. The body leads the mind into a calm focus that insulates it from random thoughts and disorder. In this state of mind and body, you feel a sense of well-being and euphoria. This state, gained whenever we practice, provides a respite from our hurried life—this is the sanctuary of Tai Chi.

Rider Insights about Healing

I'd like to share the stories of three riders.

Rider Insight, Lolly: "I've dealt with carpal tunnel syndrome in both wrists for nearly fifteen years, and my right hand is more severely affected. As this condition set in, simple tasks that involved thumb or wrist strength, such as holding a pen to write, and all gripping actions became increasingly difficult and painful. I was losing flexibility and range of motion. My doctor gave me two options—surgery or braces. So I began wearing the braces at night, but they were cumbersome and uncomfortable, and they did very little for me. If I slept without the braces, however, my sleep was interrupted several times each night by severe numbness and aching that went from my fingertips to my shoulders. I could relieve these symptoms by hanging one arm at a time over the side of the bed to help the circulation to return, but this 'cure' was itself disruptive to my sleep. I still didn't want to have surgery, but I began to feel that I was running out of options.*

"Then I met James Shaw while attending his Tai Chi for Equestrians clinic. Upon discovering his knowledge of the Chinese healing arts, and his genuinely friendly and caring manner, I knew he could offer me some suggestions. James led me through an exercise—Wrist Shaking—that nearly dropped me to my knees. I'm not a person overly sensitive to pain. I've delivered two healthy, robust boys through natural childbirth without drugs. I always thought if I could endure that, I could endure just about anything. But this exercise was quite extraordinary.

"James led me through the exercise three or four times. As my familiarity with the motions increased, I was able to put more effort into being more precise. As I released the energy from my arms as James instructed, it felt as though fire shot down my wrists and out my fingertips. That's when my knees started to buckle and I nearly cried out from the pain. James explained this pain was due to the tendons in my arms stretching and then relaxing, similar to the stretching and relaxing of a rubber band. He explained that wearing the braces only immobilized the tendons, which was just the opposite of what needed to be done.

"That initial pain was worth it. One year later I am not wearing braces; my hands and forearms do not go numb nor do they ache. The strength and range of motion in my forearms and wrists has returned. I did continue to wear the braces for a few nights after the clinic. During my daily activities I felt no pain, but a warm tingling in my hands and forearms that was pleasant, which indicated to me that healing was taking place. I decided to stop wearing the braces and I found that the numbness and pain was greatly reduced, eventually just fading away completely. I am so grateful that I met James. I am convinced that without his techniques my hands and arms would have just continued to become more weakened, stiff, and painful until I could have no longer done what I love to do—work with my Haflingers."

Rider Insight, Silke: "I have been riding for thirty years, and due to the amount of riding I have done, my back has suffered tremendously. For the last five years I have had to rely heavily on painkillers on a daily basis. I went to James's clinic without expectations. What I got was priceless. With the help of James's breathing techniques I was able to relax my lower back while riding, and my pain has since disappeared. I have not taken painkillers since that weekend in November 2000."

Rider Insight, Anne: "My husband Ed attended your clinic this past weekend and could not say enough about how much he enjoyed it. He asked if you might send him the tape of your healing movements that you showed him at the clinic. He had not been able to turn his head at all, to either side prior to the clinic, without experiencing great pain. And with just the short time you spent working with him, he is now pain-free and the range of motion in his neck and shoulders has increased dramatically."

Tai Chi and Longevity

I'll share some guidelines for older riders. One of the goals of Tai Chi is to attain longevity and live in an "eternal spring"—when life awakens anew from its winter slumber, soft and bending, vigorously stretching to the light.

In the many years that I have been traveling and working with equestrians, what most touches and saddens my heart is seeing a rider whose body is bent, stiffened, and plagued with pain from years of riding against the greater force of the horse. Just as one of the most important goals of Tai Chi is longevity in life, one of the most important goals of this book is to supply riders of all ages with the tools for longevity in riding. I believe that I will ride better at 70 than I do at 40, and I expect to have more energy when I finish a ride than before I started. My own Tai Chi teacher, who's now in her seventies, practices daily and maintains a rigorous teaching schedule.

The slow, rhythmic nature of the forms creates grace and balance in the body of all who practice, old or young. The curative benefits are well-known and have been the focus of many studies. In those who practice regularly, the strength of the bones and muscles are increased, and the functions of the metabolic, cardiovascular, and respiratory systems are improved. It is the nature of Tai Chi, as well as the human body, to have the bones carry the force of gravity and any other outside force applied to the body, through the body into the earth, our supreme support. In doing so, the bones are strengthened throughout your lifetime. In addition, Tai Chi practitioners enjoy improved balance and agility. A 1995 Washington University School of Medicine study concluded that Tai Chi practice decreases the likelihood of fall-related injuries in the elderly by as much as 25 percent.

There are many studies that I could cite that demonstrate that Tai Chi is one of the best forms of exercise to improve your life and riding. But my wish is that you prove it to yourself through the practice of the art.

My words get you no closer to your truth. If you or someone you know suffers from the difficulties that arise from an aging body trapping a young mind, please introduce them to the exercises in this book or find a Tai Chi class near you. You *can* turn back the clock; it's never too late.

Selecting a Teacher

I have been a student for virtually my whole life, and I have been a teacher for more than twenty-five years. I offer these guidelines in selecting a teacher:

1 Always have a teacher who has a teacher.

2 There are only three things a student can give to a Master (teacher): practice, service, and money. If, at any time, either service or money becomes more important than practice, the teacher has lost his way, and the student should move on.

These two simple rules can save you time, money, and heartache.

Frequent Questions and Answers

In this section, I'll address some of the questions I frequently get asked in my clinics about Tai Chi and horsemanship, and about Tai Chi as a martial art.

When I'm riding and everything is going well, it is easy to stay in balance. When things aren't going quite so well, I start to try to get it right again and it all falls apart. Is there a place that I can look to in my body to find that balance again?

Yes, there is such a place in your body: your *center*. This is a very interesting question not in the sense that you were balanced, lost your balance, and then found it difficult to regain. To me the word "try" is the key to understanding the root cause of this difficulty. Often it is the trying that keeps us out of center.

We bring all our habits, unconscious and conscious, to the saddle. If, in trying to regain your balance, you forget and slip into your unconscious habits and away from the connection you obviously had when "things were going well," you will only frustrate yourself and your horse. Remember that the *path* is mind–breath–body. The *result* is a balanced connection with your horse, not the other way around. You need to be able to let go of what you had—whether near balance, or complete imbalance—in order to find a new, real balance. What's crucial to remember is that balance comes *after* establishing the union of mind, breath, and body.

This is actually very simple—not easy, but simple. You must stay present in your body and return to the path: first you find your breath, next move it down into your center, then find your rhythm—and *then* you can find your balance.

We ride with our minds as well as our bodies, and the two are inseparable. One influences the other for better or for worse. If your horse is acting up and your focus is exclusively on his behavior, you cannot focus on your body—you are disconnected. On the other hand, if you become too focused on the position of your body on the outside, your mind detaches and becomes unaware of what is going on inside your body. You lose connection not only with your body, but also with your horse.

I am right-handed, and when I track left, my left seat doesn't contact my horse correctly—as though on the left side I have no horse to sit on. What's going on and how do I fix this?

The root of this problem is in the left/right imbalance in your body. Your right side is the dominate side, and it therefore unconsciously wants to control and lead. When tracking left the left side of the body must lead, and the right side must follow. The solution is to let go and release the right side in order to help the left to take over and lead. Controlling this sort of release is difficult until you first gain conscious control of the body in this area. You can gain this control by practicing these exercises unmounted: *Spread Your Chest* (p. 126), *Thrust Palm in Bow Stance* (p. 146), and *Hip Circles* (p. 142).

When this challenge comes up on horseback, you can work on this as follows, using the path of mind—breath—body. First, become aware of the tension in the right side of your body. Second, soften and release this tension through abdominal breathing; visualize it dropping down through the bones of your body, then down through your horse, and finally into the ground. Now track left and turn your belly button to the right as you move to the left. This places the left side of your body in the lead position and moves the right back slightly to follow.

My horse is constantly falling out of the gait he's in. Why does this happen?

I have seen this happen many times and I have heard the rider claim that her horse is lazy and does not like to work. I believe that in most cases the horse is more confused than lazy, and he would love to work if the rider's weight was not constantly shifting forward onto the horse's forehand.

Let me explain: I often see a rider ask for the trot from a poorly balanced position. When the horse responds and picks up the trot, the rider is ill-prepared to follow the new larger motion of the animal. If, through habit she is slightly ahead of the horse's movement (she does this to feel safe), the added momentum caused by the horse's increased motion pushes her body weight even more forward. If her weight drops to the front of her seat, it slows the movement in the pelvis, thus telling the horse to stop or slow. On the other hand, if through tension her weight does not drop down, it must then go up and forward, getting transferred through leverage into the horse's forehand, causing discomfort and a mixed message. The horse, not surprisingly, often falls out of the gait at this point.

Now, I'm sure that there are times when the horse is a problem. My focus is always on the rider. Only after I'm sure it's not the rider do I look to the horse.

My horse has a habit of jerking his head and neck forward, trying to pull against me.

Your horse jerks you forward to get your weight off his back. There may be other reasons for this pulling, but for our purposes we will assume the root problem is in your seat.

When you sit on a horse's back you take on a great responsibility because you're sitting on the horse's weakest part, right in the middle of his spine, and directly over his center. Structurally, that's the weakest part of his body. He has more structural strength over his feet at the withers and hindquarters.

Think about the mechanics of your position on the horse. You sit in a comfortable place. The horse has greater strength and motion at the shoulders and hips. You're joining centers at the place of least motion on the horse's spine. This is the nature of the center—that it moves the least and every motion that comes from the center moves out from the center.

Many times I have seen riders get pulled out of the saddle as the horse throws his head forward, jerking the reins. When the rider loses her seat, it allows the horse to stop. The rider then sits back into the saddle and tells the horse to walk, then trot, and the jerking starts immediately. Somehow the blame gets put on the horse, when in my opinion the cause is the rider's seat. Of course if this action and reaction continues for any length of time, it can become a habit in the horse. Whether or not this pulling has become routine, the solution lies in the rider's seat.

I have been having trouble getting my horse to collect. What's wrong?

When a horse collects and rounds his back, the spine is softened and he is more comfortable to sit on. A horse will only do this if the rider's seat allows it in a manner that's comfortable for the horse. If your seat is not soft, it will constantly push against the horse's back at the wrong moments, and he will not offer his back in collection. Too often I see a rider using the reins, spurs, and whip in an effort to aid in collection before the rider is truly ready, meaning that her position is in opposition to the horse's back. As you know, horses' backs are sensitive. The horse will give you his back when your invitation to him is equally sensitive.

The required "sensitive" invitation involves more than just having a mechanically correct seat. You must have centered yourself and then joined centers with your horse by *opening your gates*. It is my experience that a horse will only connect with you to the degree that you can open your Eight Gates. The rider's gates correspond to the horse's. Your Heart gates align with your upper back, and so do the horse's. If they are closed, the horse's will also be closed. Once you open, he can open, and his back will come to you.

I've seen riders who are quite accomplished at opening all the gates except their Front and Back of the Heart gates. This is usually tied to protecting themselves emotionally in other areas of their lives. When they let go of the fear of being hurt and really open their hearts to the horse, the level of collection and connection that follows is remarkable.

I have a hard time sitting trot extensions. What do you suggest?

The extended trot creates a great deal of energy coming up through the horse's back, and it also increases the time that you must follow. (Review *Follow—Match—Lead*, p. 168.) These changes often cause the rider to "hold on," and in doing so, close the Back of the Heart gate as the breath rises in the body. Note that the holding may only affect the breath and not be seen in the physical body as clenching or tightening. The holding in the body is hidden in the cervical–thoracic junction of the spine. The key here is to open the Back of the Heart by expanding the breath back and out. By so doing you can allow the latissimus dorsi muscles to hold the shoulders down, pulling the energy back into the seat. Your goal is to expand and connect with your horse rather than tighten and push away.

I have a green horse. How can Tai Chi benefit my training?

I have many students whose job entails starting young green horses. The greatest bene-fit of Tai Chi for them is the sense of calm and physical balance gained from the prac-tice of this program. If there is one thing a young horse needs, it's a leader both on the ground and in the saddle. The key to developing a relationship of mutual respect on the ground is clear communication without force, and the same is true in the saddle. Tai Chi provides the training for clear, balanced communication without force.

My horse is hot. How can Tai Chi affect him?

The most direct way that Tai Chi helps a hot horse is through the calm and controlled abdominal breathing you develop. When you're on the back of a hot horse, very often your breath is short and up high in your chest. Breathing in this way brings your energy up, and this brings the horse's up as well. By staying calm and balanced, you can direct the heat of the horse in a positive, controlled direction.

Are there variations of Tai Chi?

Yes, there are many different styles of Tai Chi taught in the U.S. Some styles are more physically demanding than others, such as the Chen and Wu styles. Other styles are taught as a motion-meditation or a no-impact form of exercise. Whatever style you choose, your teacher should be able to demonstrate and explain the martial applica-tion of all the postures. This basis is what makes the practice real and it works to improve your riding skill. Otherwise, the movements are just another form of exercise.

How can I learn Tai Chi—should I take a class?

There is no substitute for a great teacher. There are many books and videotapes avail-able (my video, *Tai Chi for the Equestrian*, being one of them), but just as in riding, you must acquire the feel of it all by practicing, which I believe is best done in person with an instructor. Books and tapes are helpful references, for motions, underlying principles, and history; they can be valuable supplements to one-on-one or a group instruction.

Do I need a trained Tai Chi instructor to incorporate Tai Chi into my riding?

No, not necessarily. With the help of this book, you should be able to take what you learn and apply it successfully to your riding. However, if you are interested in "really" learning Tai Chi—that is, learning it for more than solely using it in your riding program—then yes, I would encourage you to find a qualified Tai Chi instructor in your area.

Can Tai Chi cause injury?

While the slow and relaxed nature of the movements of Tai Chi rarely causes injuries, there is always the possibility for something unexpected to happen. The most common complaint is that of a sore back after a long period of practice. I have found through my own experience and that of others that back pain usually involves two factors: (1) there is a preexisting condition in the back, and (2) the positions are not being done properly.

If the proper alignment of the bones is not maintained, the stress of gravity will inevitably take its toll on the back. Old injuries and developed compensations in the body can be healed and retrained through the practice of Tai Chi. I would recommend that you follow the guidance of an experienced teacher.

I'm a disabled rider. How can I adapt the exercises?

I have had the pleasure of working with many handicapped and disabled riders, and together we've had great success at modifying motions to suit individual needs. While I can't say specifically how to modify any one particular exercise for every person's disability, here are some guidelines to follow.

Always focus on slow, deep breathing directed by the mind.

I once worked with a group of disabled riders in Washington state. One of the riders suffered from cerebral palsy. The left side of her body was greatly affected, so much so that she could not lift her arm and had minimal movement in the fingers and hand on that side. For the exercise *Thrust Palm in Bow Stance* (p. 146). I asked her just to imagine that her left arm was raised and the palm pushing out. She did so, and as she returned to the center position, her eyes were lit up and her face was full of excitement. She told me that she could feel the electricity flowing through her arm and into her hand as she focused and directed her mind and chi.

All of the upper body motions may be done from a wheelchair.

Most of the mounted work can be done by a disabled rider if closely directed by a qualified handicapped riding instructor. I have also had the pleasure of meeting and working with a riding instructor and horseman who, as a result of injury, lost the use of his legs fifteen years ago. Almost immediately he "got back on the horse," and he has learned how to ride without the use of his legs. That means that he rides from his center. Without the leverage and active weight supplied by the muscles in his legs, all his aids must come from his seat. Although our language is slightly different, through conversation we have discovered that he has done on his own out of necessity many of the things that I have taught you. By learning and following the principles and theories in this book, you can ride more by doing less.

How does Tai Chi differ from Yoga?

There are far more similarities between Tai Chi and yoga than there are differences. Both focus the mind exclusively on the body and develop mind and body harmony through movement and breath control. Both seek to create and move that invisible life force energy within the human body. In Tai Chi it's called chi, and in yoga, it's called prana.

The major difference between the two is that Tai Chi is a martial art and therefore bound by different laws. During the practice of Tai Chi, you are always aware that there is an opponent trying to uproot your balance by any means possible. So in Tai Chi practice you never negate gravity by sitting or lying on the ground. In a form, you also never use gravity alone to stretch the body. You always use an opposing muscle group to create the stretch. Yoga is a fantastic mind and body exercise that I myself practice. Remember, variety is the spice of life, or as the Buddha said, "Many roads lead to enlightenment."

Acknowledgments

I'd like to thank the people of Trafalgar Square Publishing: Caroline Robbins, Publisher, and Martha Cook, Managing Editor, for their patience and support from the beginning—and most of all, for asking me to write this book.

Chris Bray, writer/editor and friend: thank you for your hours editing and your research in and out of the saddle. Your personal experience of the work has added greatly to this book. Thanks to Charlene Strickland, writer/editor.

My sisters, Becky Stanzyk and Cynthia Thomas, for your unconditional love and guidance throughout my whole life.

My good friends and riding instructors:
Dr. Susan Connors: from day one you have embraced and made this work your own, and by doing so, have taken it to a level I would not have reached without you. Thank you for your guidance, knowledge and most of all friendship.

Missy Hicks, Gayle Smith, Kay Kamish, Suzi Hoffman Peacock, Jute Heinerson, Alexander Kurland: thank you for unselfishly sharing your knowledge of riding and horses with me and for letting me in. We've only scratched the surface. Linda Rogers, for your early support of my work and our friendship.

Betsy Steiner, my friend and teacher: thank you for all you have done and continue to do for me. You introduced me to riding with our first article, and before I ever sat on a horse you foresaw the benefits of Tai Chi for the riding world. I am forever grateful.

My Lau Kune Do Brothers: Joseph Lavitt, Dan Brewer, George Gains, Chris Hendrix, Fred Payne—who never lowered the bar and taught me that when the mind and body are exhausted, it is the Spirit that endures the last miles.

Richard Tsim, for your early guidance on this journey and for providing the sanctuary of the temple in which I, and countless others, could grow to our own heights.

Wen Mei-Yu, for sharing with me your incredible knowledge of the inner workings of Tai Chi and being a living example that grace, beauty, and power arise from the same source deep within the human spirit.

Tim Cartmel, one of the greatest martial artists and teachers I've had the pleasure to meet—thanks for keeping it all very real.

Paul Wiederman: thank you, my brother, for being a constant source of creative inspiration and encouragement. See you at Boodle Hole.

Bill W., Dr. Bob, and friends, for picking me up at the bottom and giving me the spiritual tools by which to live this new life.

Janice Bear, for her mystic foresight and the gift of "walking backward."

Mary Trost: thank you for your constant love and support of me at every level.

Dr. Syng Ku Yu, for sharing your life's work of healing with me and encouraging me to follow my own path.

Cele and Tony Nobel, for your constant love and support from the very start. Thank you, oh "Keepers of the Tree."

Sharon Shaw: You were the first to say, "You can do this, and it will be great." Thank you for your love and encouragement.

My four-legged "Masters": these are the true masters of riding and healing. Thank you for choosing me and enriching my life beyond compare.

There are many more people to whom I owe a dept of gratitude, especially all who have participated in my workshops, clinics, and lectures. I wouldn't be able to do this work without you.

Appendix A

Summary of Exercises in This Book

Summary of Exercises

Chapter 1: Tai Chi and Horsemanship
Lays the groundwork for applying Tai Chi to riding.

Chapter 2: Fundamentals of Tai Chi: An Ancient Art, A New Perspective
Introduces the Eight Principles that guide Tai Chi practice and the Eight Gates that affect the flow of chi in the rider's body.

Chapter 3: Your Mind: Awakening Self-Awareness and the Creative Mind

Exercises	Purpose	Routine	When to Move On
Standing Meditation and Sitting Meditation	The most basic position in which to develop the mind/body connection while maintaining structural alignment of the bones. Practicing these exercises plants the seed of quiet awareness that all other exercises build on.	These exercises can be practiced any time you have a moment to focus inward and should be practiced for a few minutes every morning before you start your day. I recommend 2 to 5 minutes of *Standing Meditation* before you ride for at least 2 weeks, after that, the time it takes to get the benefit can be achieved in less than a minute.	After 2 weeks of practice and when you have felt the change in your body described in the Ah Ha! section of this exercise.
Side Step	*Side Step* first challenges you to maintain the mind/body connection achieved in *Standing Meditation* while moving your body. The slow, subtle shift of weight that takes place by engaging the pelvis not only creates sensitivity of the seat, but also brings to the surface the unconscious physical limitations of the pelvis that you will overcome through practice.	Initially, *Side Step* should be practiced 5 times every time you do *Standing Meditation*. During your first 2 weeks of practice you will most likely find yourself practicing the shift of weight throughout your day—this is the intent. Moving in this way should become a part of your life, not just something you do as an exercise before you ride. When this happens, you may reduce the practice to just before you ride.	After 2 weeks of practice and when you have felt the change in your body described in the Ah Ha! section of this exercise.
Wrist Shaking	The purpose of this exercise is two-fold: (1) to make you aware of the internal energy of the body (chi), and (2) to help you check your progress in the physical balancing of your body in regard to the inseparable role the bones and muscles play in maintaining balance in motion.	A few moments of *Wrist Shaking* after *Side Step* is sufficient in the first 2 weeks. Remember, *Wrist Shaking* is done to check your progress in your overall mind/body balance.	After 2 weeks of practice and when you have felt the change in your body described in the Ah Ha! section of this exercise.

Tai Chi

Exercises	Purpose	Routine	When to Move On
Sink and Circulate the Chi	The purpose of this exercise is to begin to match the movements of your body with the rhythm of your breath while maintaining the mind/body connection.	5 repetitions of *Sink and Circulate the Chi* after *Wrist Shaking* is sufficient during the first 2 weeks. With this amount of practice you will begin to find that you are connecting your breath to the movements of your body throughout your day. Bravo!	After 2 weeks of practice and when you have felt the change in your body described in the Ah Ha! section of this exercise.
Horse Stance and Wall Sitting	The purpose of this exercise is to develop leg strength and train the body to open the second gate (Ming Meng) while negotiating the force of gravity through the body.	I recommend doing 5 repetitions every day. If this is too much, I would recommend that it be done a minimum of 3 repetitions, 3 times a week. This is one of the most valuable exercises in this book; I also realize it's the most physically challenging. If you do it, you will be able to access your Ming Meng in a very short time.	After 2 weeks of practice and when you have felt the change in your body described in the Ah Ha! section of this exercise.
Walking Backward	This exercise teaches you to move with balance and rhythm.	Do this exercise as often as possible, or at least 3 times a week for one month. Performing the exercise for 5 to 15 minutes at a time is ideal.	This exercise should become a part of your routine for the rest of your life.

Tai Chi

Chapter 4: Expanding Our Perspective: Tai Chi's Healing Path and the Gift of the Horse

Laing Gong Palm and Fist	This seemingly simple exercise is contained in every Laing Gong exercise except one (*Hold the Sky with Both Hands*). It functions to pump chi throughout the arms and hands. It is very effective at reducing the amount of tension that is unconsciously held in the hand. This exercise is also used to start to heal pain and stiffness in the hands.	To start, spend a few minutes a day practicing opening and closing the hand into the Laing Gong Palm and Fist. The time varies with each person, but with practice you should very soon see a change in the color of the palm, that is, white spots will appear in the palm and fingers.	Practice until you can easily open the hand, keep the fingers together, and "hollow" the palm of the hand.

Laing Gong

Chi Gong

Chapter 5: Your Breath: Learning to Breathe and Connect with Your Horse

Exercises	Purpose	Routine
Abdominal Breathing	The purpose of this exercise is to retrain the body to allow for the expansion of the center (abdomen). The exercise also lowers the rider's center of balance from the chest to the waist, and it teaches you to open the first gate (Dain Tian).	As with all the breath work in this chapter, you can practice anytime you become aware of your breath. After becoming competent with the exercise, 5 repetitions, 3 times a day is a good start. This should be completed in about one minute's time. When mounted, try spending the first few minutes of your time in the saddle focused on this breathing. Keep doing this exercise until you catch yourself breathing correctly more often than not. The goal of all breath work is to not have to think about it.
Counting Your Breath	The purpose of this exercise is to bring into the conscious mind the rhythm of your breath and learn how it affects your movement.	Anytime during the day that you become aware of your breath, spend a few moments finding your rhythm by counting your breath. When mounted, practice for one minute after completing *Abdominal Breathing.*
Open the Ming Meng	This exercise creates free movement in the lower back and spine. The exercise also teaches you to open the second gate (Ming Meng).	Practice anytime you become aware of your breath. After becoming competent with the exercise, 5 repetitions, 3 times a day is a good start. Try *Open the Ming Meng* at night before you go to sleep while lying on your back in bed. Many people have found this to be effective. This should be completed in about one minute's time. In the saddle, do 5 minutes of focused practice every time you ride.
Embracing the Moon	This exercise connects the upper body to the lower body. The exercise removes tension from the chest and arms, and teaches you to open the third and fourth gates (the *Front and Back of the Heart*).	As with all the breath work in this chapter, you can practice anytime you become aware of your breath. After becoming competent with the exercise, 5 repetitions, 3 times a day is a good start. This should be completed in about 2 to 3 minutes time.
Heaven and Earth	This exercise teaches you to use the upper body while staying connected to the lower. The exercise also connects you to the earth and heavens energetically, and it trains the mind to keep the first four gates open while moving.	
Breathing to a Halt or Walk	The purpose of this exercise is to begin to actively use your breath as an aid.	

Chapter 6: Your Body: Enhancing Your Movement and Power

Chapter 7: Application: Bringing It All Together in the Saddle

Teaches you to apply what you've learned to the gaits, transitions, bending, lateral movements, and jumping.

Chapter 8: The Road Continues: Health and Tai Chi

Shows how to use Tai Chi to improve your health, and includes frequently asked questions and answers.

Appendix B

Anatomical Diagrams

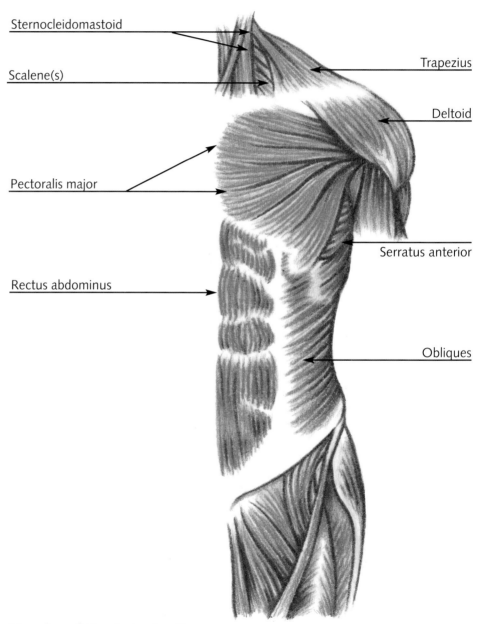

Sternocleidomastoid

Scalene(s)

Pectoralis major

Rectus abdominus

Trapezius

Deltoid

Serratus anterior

Obliques

Muscles of the Anterior Torso

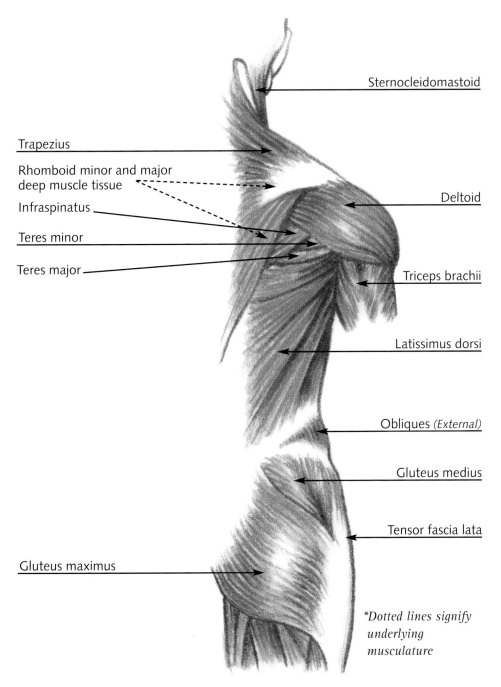

Sternocleidomastoid

Trapezius

Rhomboid minor and major
deep muscle tissue

Infraspinatus

Deltoid

Teres minor

Teres major

Triceps brachii

Latissimus dorsi

Obliques (External)

Gluteus medius

Tensor fascia lata

Gluteus maximus

*Dotted lines signify
underlying
musculature

Muscles of the Posterior Torso

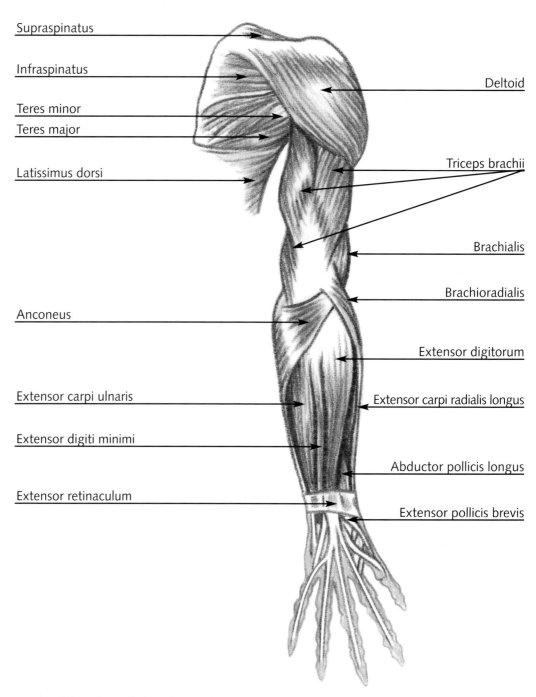

Supraspinatus

Infraspinatus

Teres minor

Teres major

Latissimus dorsi

Anconeus

Extensor carpi ulnaris

Extensor digiti minimi

Extensor retinaculum

Deltoid

Triceps brachii

Brachialis

Brachioradialis

Extensor digitorum

Extensor carpi radialis longus

Abductor pollicis longus

Extensor pollicis brevis

Muscles of the Posterior Arm

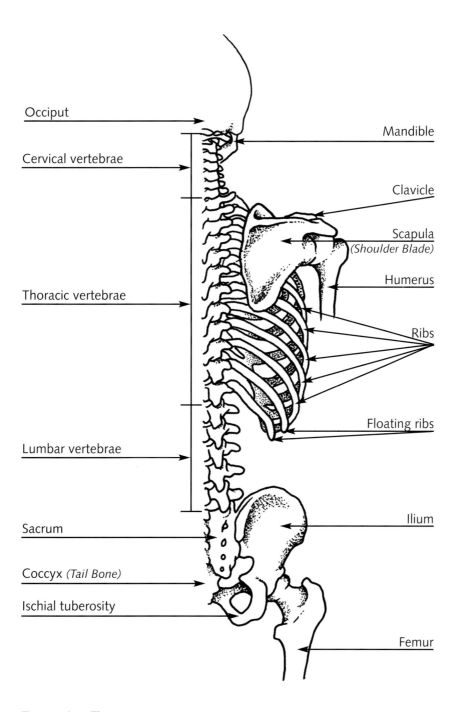

Occiput

Cervical vertebrae

Thoracic vertebrae

Lumbar vertebrae

Sacrum

Coccyx *(Tail Bone)*

Ischial tuberosity

Mandible

Clavicle

Scapula
(Shoulder Blade)

Humerus

Ribs

Floating ribs

Ilium

Femur

Posterior Torso

Yin

H	= Heart
P	= Pericardium
L	= Lungs
Liv	= Liver
SP	= Spleen
CV	= Conception vessel
K	= Kidney

Yang

Li	= Large intestine
TW	= Triple warmer
Si	= Small intestine
St	= Stomach
GB	= Gall bladder
B	= Bladder
GV	= Governing vessel

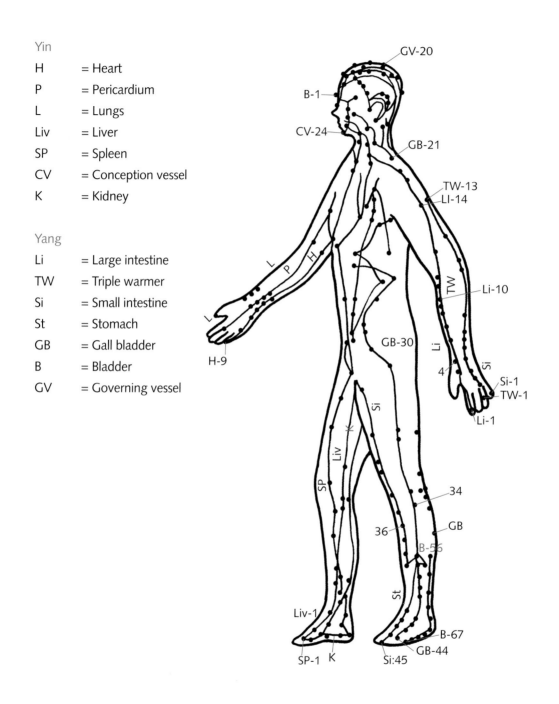

Yin and Yang Meridians

Appendix C

Resources

Web Sites

www.shawtaichi.com

> This is my own web site; you can find out more about me and my work here including upcoming clinics and events, videos, and more. (You can also contact me directly at taishawchi@aol.com.)

www.shenwu.com

> Tim Cartmell's web site, the best martial artist I've ever seen. Tim has had a great influence on my teaching. He teaches the truth without any secrets or mysticism. Tim's site also has a great deal of information on various martial arts and links to other resources.

www.thinkfit.com

> Paul Widerman's web site, creator of Smart Bells™, an innovative replacement for dumb bells. If you need to increase your strength, Smart Bells™ are the way to go.

www.wenmeiyu.com

> Wen Mei Yu is a Tai Chi Grandmaster and my teacher. She is a great inspiration as a martial artist and a person. There are many links from this web site to the world of Tai Chi and other martial arts.

Bibliography and Further Reading

Andrews, Ted. *Animal Speak*. St. Paul, Minnesota: Llewellyn Publications, 1993.

Benfield, Harriet, L.Ac., and Korngold, Efrem, L.Ac., O.M.D. *Between Heaven and Earth: A Guide to Chinese Medicine*. New York: Ballantine Books, 1991.

Berk, William R. *Chinese Healing Arts*. Unique Publications, 1986.

Cartmell, Tim. *Effortless Combat Throws*. High View Publications, 1996.

Choa Kok Sui. *Advanced Pranic Healing*. York Beach, Maine: Samuel Weiser, Inc., 1995.

Collinge, William, Ph.D. *Subtle Energy*. New York: Warner Books, 1998.

Deng Ming-Dao. *365 Tao Daily Meditations*. San Francisco: Harper Collins, 1992.

Loa Tsu. *Tao Te Ching*. Translated by Gia-Fu Feng and Jane English. New York: Random House, 1972.

Miyamoto Musashi. *The Book of Five Rings*. Translated by Thomas Cleary. Boston: Shambhala Publications, 1993.

Rawson, Philip, and Legeza, Laszlo. *Tao: The Chinese Philosophy of Time and Change*. London: Thames and Hudson, 1973.

Schusdziarra, H, M.D., and Schusdziarra, V. *An Anatomy of Riding*. Breakthrough Publications, Inc., 1978.

Storm, Hyemeyohsts. *Seven Arrows*. New York: Ballantine Books, 1972.

Sun Tzu. *The Art of War*. Translated by Samuel B. Griffith. Oxford: Oxford University Press, 1971.

Swift, Sally. *Centered Riding*. North Pomfret, Vermont: Trafalgar Square Publishing, 1985.

Thich Nhat Hanh. *Breath! You Are Alive*. Berkeley: Parallax Press, 1996.

Thich Nhat Hanh. *The Miracle of Mindfulness*. Boston: Beacon Press, 1975.

Waysun Liao. *Tai Chi Classics*. Boston: Shambhala Publications, 1990.

Wu Ying-hua, and Ma Yueh-liang. *Wu Style Taichichuan*. Shanghai Book Company, 1993.

Xie Peiqi. *Guiding Energy Sitting Meditations*. Toronto: Traditional Studies Press, 1995.

Yeshi Donden. *Health Through Balance: An Introduction to Tibetan Medicine*. Ithaca, New York: Snow Lion Publications, 1986.

Index

Page numbers in *italic* indicate illustrations.